Problems in American Civilization

UNDER THE EDITORIAL DIRECTION OF *George Rogers Taylor*

THE PULLMAN BOYCOTT OF 1894

THE PROBLEM OF FEDERAL INTERVENTION

THE PULLMAN BOYCOTT OF 1894
THE PROBLEM OF FEDERAL
INTERVENTION

EDITED WITH AN INTRODUCTION BY
Colston E. Warne

Problems in American Civilization

D. C. HEATH AND COMPANY: Boston

INTRODUCTION

THE Pullman strike of 1894 at its inception was a dispute between a stong-minded individualist, George M. Pullman, and the 4000 workers employed in his railway car manufacturing plant at Pullman, Illinois, just south of Chicago. Behind this strike were the familiar issues of wages and union recognition. The workers, disturbed by repeated wage cuts which had ensued during the panic of 1893, had organized a union which, in turn, had affiliated with the newly-formed American Railway Union. The latter organization, led by Eugene V. Debs, was designed to bring all railway workers into a single industrial union to enhance their bargaining position.

The strike at Pullman, Illinois, was indeed so peaceful, so undramatic, and so unsuccessful in attaining its objectives, that, after sixty years, it would undoubtedly be considered as a minor episode in the turbulent labor history of Chicago, had it not tripped off a major railway dispute on the railways radiating from Chicago. Out of the heated conflict over the American Railway Union boycott of Pullman cars emerged a significant controversy between the President of the United States and the Governor of Illinois over the use of Federal troops without state consent in an industrial conflict. The Pullman boycott was to be the occasion for the issuance of a blanket injunction by the Federal government, restraining union leaders from interfering with railway operation. This injunction was deemed by labor to be a judicial "Gatling gun" under which the leaders of labor could be jailed.

Few episodes in American labor history have been featured by such partisanship. Sides were taken by mayors of cities and governors of states. The President of the United States and his Attorney General were to become central participants in the controversy. Newspapers were violently partisan. It seemed as if the Pullman boycott split the nation into warring camps, and raised the cries of "government by injunction" and of "anarchy," cries which continued long after the fight ended.

While the issues in the initial dispute at Pullman, Illinois, are of more than ordinary interest, these are given rather cursory treatment in the readings in order that central attention may focus upon the Pullman boycott which brought retaliation from the Chicago carriers and a subsequent wave of sympathetic strikes.

In order that the major events may be more easily disentangled in the accounts which follow, the chronology of the Pullman strike is given below.

1880	George M. Pullman built the model factory town of Pullman, Illinois.
1886	The General Managers' Association was formed as a voluntary unincorporated association of 24 railways centering or terminating in Chicago. In 1893, this Association began to unify employer wage policies by establishing a standard Chicago scale for switchmen.

June 20, 1893	The American Railway Union was founded under the leadership of Eugene V. Debs to unite railway labor in a single organization.	July 2	A Federal injunction was issued (served on July 3 and July 4). This injunction enjoined A.R.U. leaders from "compelling or inducing by threats, intimidation, persuasion, force or violence, railway employees to refuse or fail to perform their duties."
September, 1893–May, 1894	Wages in the Pullman Works were reduced, on the average by 25 per cent.		
March, April, 1894	Workers in Pullman's Palace Car Company joined the American Railway Union.	July 3	Federal troops entered the dispute.
May 7, 9	A committee of Pullman workers waited on management but received no concessions, either in the form of increased wages or lowered rents.	July 5, 6	Governor Altgeld of Illinois protested the use of Federal troops and was answered by President Cleveland.
		July 7	The principal officers of the A.R.U. were arrested, indicted, and held under $10,000 bail.
May 10	Three of the committee were laid off, allegedly for lack of work. That evening Pullman workers voted to strike.	July 12	An AFL meeting in Chicago refused to authorize sympathetic action. The A.R.U. unsuccessfully offered to abandon the strike, provided that the workers were rehired without prejudice, except where convicted of crime.
May 11	Pullman works closed.		
June 9–26	The American Railway Union convened in Chicago, representing 465 local unions and a claimed membership of 150,000.		
		August 2	Pullman works reopened. Strike ended. Local leaders were not rehired.
June 15, 22	The Pullman Company refused to receive any communication from the American Railway Union or to permit five proposed arbitrators to determine whether there was anything to arbitrate.	August 15	Hearings of U. S. Strike Commission began in Chicago.
June 21	Delegates of A.R.U. voted to stop handling Pullman cars on June 26th unless the Pullman Company agreed to arbitration.		
June 22	The Pullman Company met with the General Managers' Association and reached an agreement to resist the proposed boycott.		
June 26	The boycott and accompanying strikes began and spread rapidly as General Managers' Association members discharged men who refused to switch passenger trains with Pullman cars.		

From the above, it will be observed that the local disagreement over wage rates became, a little more than a month later, a national railway dispute. For some years, both labor and capital on the railroads had been heading toward such a test of strength. The railroads, overbuilt, overcapitalized, and faced with a falling price level, were in no mood to yield to A.R.U. pressure. Railway executives feared the rising tide of labor organization and especially the unifying efforts of Debs, who sought to knit the separate railway crafts into a single union. Labor, resentful because of wage cuts and unemployment, developed unexpected solidarity and bitterness toward management. Pullman, Illinois, was the spark which set off an already-pending dispute.

Because the Pullman struggle came to involve so many issues of basic policy, it is well to identify at the outset some of the major disagreements, even though some of these will, because of space limitations, receive little emphasis. (1) *Individual vs. collective bargaining:* Was George Pullman correct in adhering strongly to the principle of individual bargaining – the establishment of wages without recourse to negotations with a union of his employees? (2) *The model town:* Was the town of Pullman, Illinois, an unsound experiment in paternalism? Or was it a genuine attempt to improve the living standards of workers? Was Pullman as landlord to be distinguished from Pullman as employer? (3) *Industrial unionism:* Was the central idea of the American Railway Union – that of uniting in one organization all workers associated with the railway industry – a sound one? Or was the existing craft union structure (with separate unions for the engineers, the firemen, the trainmen, and the conductors) more adequate? Moreover, quite apart from the merit of industrial unionism on the railways, should such a railway union reach out to bargain for workers in a manufacturing plant providing railway equipment? (4) *The Pullman boycott:* Did members of the American Railway Union and their sympathizers on the railways have a legal or moral right to launch a boycott of Pullman cars in order to support the strikers at Pullman, Illinois? (5) *The right of public utility employees to strike:* Did railway employees have the right to quit work in sympathy with striking Pullman employees, irrespective of the effect of their action upon the nation at large? (6) *The right of Federal intervention:* Faced with a strike, should the railway companies

have been allowed to deputize nonstriking employees as marshals? Was the Federal injunction warranted in the terms in which it was granted? Was Governor Altgeld of Illinois correct in affirming that outcrops of violence, under the Federal Constitution, should first be handled by the local and state police forces rather than by Federal troops? Or was President Cleveland on sound ground in calling in the Army? (7) *Arbitration:* Finally, was the whole dispute one in which arbitration should have played a crucial role? Or was Pullman correct in insisting from the beginning that there was nothing to arbitrate?

In order to give an over-all view of the clash of forces in 1894, the readings begin with summary articles by Samuel Gompers, President of the American Federation of Labor, and Wade Hampton, United States Commissioner of Railroads. These articles, written shortly after the defeat of the American Railway Union, serve to point up the major issues as well as to illustrate existing tensions. They are followed by an excerpt from the report of the United States Strike Commission, appointed by President Cleveland, which estimates the losses occasioned by the strike and the crimes incident to it.

The second section of the readings identifies the three principal contestants: Pullman's Palace Car Company, the American Railway Union, and the General Managers' Association. It also includes background material concerning the initial conflict at Pullman, Illinois. Brief statements are made by the two primary contestants – the Pullman Company and the local union in the Pullman works. These are followed by the Strike Commission summary of the Pullman controversy.

The third section summarizes the events of the railway boycott and sympathetic strike, conducted by the American Railway Union in the summer of 1894. The first selection includes excerpts from the report of the United States Strike Commission; the second is a selection drawn from Ray Ginger's sympathetic biography of Debs, *The Bending Cross*.

The fourth section, which is pivotal to the present problem, relates directly to Federal intervention in the dispute. This section opens with excerpts from the injunction obtained by the Federal government against Debs and his associates. This is followed by highlights of the decision of the United States Supreme Court, *In Re Debs*, which unanimously upheld the Federal position.

The next two selections, by John P. Altgeld, then Governor of Illinois, well indicate the strenuous objections which he lodged against the use of the injunction and Federal troops in the dispute. These are followed by a stout defense by President Grover Cleveland, written some years after the controversy. A rebuttal is presented by Eugene V. Debs.

The last five readings reflect differing attitudes of writers toward Federal intervention and especially toward the Debs case. Henry James defends Richard Olney, Cleveland's Attorney General, and his vigorous course of action in the dispute. Gustavus Myers finds the Supreme Court decision to be evidence of class bias, a viewpoint strongly opposed by Charles Warren. The final selections reflect more recent interpretations of the Pullman boycott. Willard L. King, prominent Chicago attorney and author of a biography of Melville Weston Fuller, Chief Justice of the United States at the time of the Debs case, draws upon his knowledge of the period to conclude that Federal intervention in the dispute was lawful and that the Debs decision was sound. In contrast, Almont Lindsey's history of the Pullman strike, published in 1942, differs markedly from King in interpreting the injunction and the subsequent court action.

After more than sixty years, the dispute over the Pullman boycott continues. To some, the episode reflected the wise and expeditious application of the Federal authority to restrain the clearly unlawful conduct of a labor leader whose actions were creating irreparable public injury. To others, the Pullman boycott was an illustration of how the Federal administration, the Federal troops, and even the Federal courts, in a period of tense labor conflict, were harnessed to serve the will of giant railway companies which were interlocked with Pullman interests. In the opinion of this latter group, Pullman's pocketbook could only be effectively reached through an effective boycott of Pullman cars.

Not a few of the issues emerging in the Pullman dispute have been singularly persistent. The place of the injunction in industries affected with a public interest remains still in controversy. We have by no means settled the question of strikes in public service enterprises. The boycott is likewise a perennial topic for legislative debate. While the nation has, through the Railway Labor Act of 1926 and the Wagner Act of 1935 (as amended by the Taft-Hartley Act), recognized the right of workers to organize and to engage in collective bargaining, it has by no means removed major labor disputes from the political orbit. Boycotts, injunctions, sympathetic strikes, "cooling-off periods," industry-wide bargaining, and compulsory arbitration still evoke intense debate. Indeed, in recent years, considerable discussion has ensued over the desirability of presidential injunctive action to terminate, for a period, paralyzing strikes in such industries as steel and coal. It is to be hoped that these readings will contribute to a better understanding of a significant chapter in our labor history and will provide some of the necessary background for analyzing still unresolved problems in the relationship of government to labor and business.

[Note: The statements quoted in the Clash of Issues on page xiv are from the following sources: Grover Cleveland, "The Government in the Chicago Strike of 1894," in *Presidential Problems* by Grover Cleveland (New York: The Century Company, 1904), pp. 116–117; Eugene V. Debs, "The Federal Government and the Chicago Strike," in *Debs: His Life, Writings and Speeches* (Chicago: Charles H. Kerr and Company, 1908), pp. 184–185 (copyrighted 1908 by The Appeal to Reason); Samuel Gompers quoted in the *North American Review*, 1894; Wade Hampton quoted in the *North American Review*, August, 1894.]

CONTENTS

UNCLE SAM: "Drop 'em, my boy, drop 'em. We'll settle our grievances at the ballot." — *Toronto World.*

What can he do, but strike back?
— *Grip, Toronto.*

STUPIDITY and GREED

AN IMPENDING DOWNFALL.

—*Ram's Horn.*

THE CLASH OF ISSUES

... in the opinion read by the learned justice, the inherent power of the Government to execute the powers and functions belonging to it by means of physical force through its official agents, and on every foot of American soil, was amply vindicated by a process of reasoning simple, logical, unhampered by fanciful distinctions, and absolutely conclusive; and the Government's peaceful resort to the court, the injunction issued in its aid, and all the proceedings thereon, including the imprisonment of Debs and his associates, were fully approved.

Thus the Supreme Court of the United States has written the closing words of this history, tragical in many of its details, and in every line provoking sober reflection. . . .

                                     — GROVER CLEVELAND

... there is available proof sufficient to make it clear to the unprejudiced mind . . . that the United States government, under the administration of President Grover Cleveland, was at the beck and call of the railroad corporations, acting as one through the "General Managers' Association," and that these corporations, with the Federal Courts and troops to back them up, had swarms of mercenaries sworn in as deputy marshals to incite violence as a pretext for taking possession of the headquarters of the American Railway Union by armed force, throwing its leaders into prison without trial and breaking down the union that was victorious, maligning, brow-beating, and persecuting its peaceable and law-abiding members, and putting the railroad corporations in supreme control of the situation.

This was the part of President Cleveland in the Chicago strike. . . .

                                     — EUGENE V. DEBS

... was it justifiable? From the standpoint of the employer, No. From the standpoint of a labor organization having an agreement with an employer whose provisions a strike would violate, No. From the standpoint of the A.R.U., having no agreement with either of the railroad companies involved, and expressing the inarticulate protest of the masses against the wrongs inflicted upon any of their brothers and their yearning for justice to all mankind, Yes; a thousand times yes.

         — SAMUEL GOMPERS, President, American Federation of Labor

I have said that this strike was inexcusable. . . . What justification can be offered for the order of the leaders of all the labor organizations in the country, connected in any manner with the railroads, that each member should at once throw up his position as evidence of sympathy with the Pullman employees?

... Every interest of the country is to be sacrificed, every vested right is to be trampled upon, every principle of law and of morals is to be violated, simply because workmen engaged in a particular business cannot obtain the wages they demand.

         — WADE HAMPTON, United States Commissioner of Railroads

DIFFERING VIEWS OF THE DISPUTE

Samuel Gompers: THE LESSON OF THE RECENT STRIKES

ON Decoration Day, May 30, 1894, Judge Grosscup, of the United States Courts, in his oration commemorative of the day, took occasion to say that "the growth of labor organizations must be checked by law," yet when the sounds of his voice had scarcely died away we had in the midst of us the greatest and most extensive labor struggle that has ever taken place among the wage-workers of America, and possibly of the world.

Thousands of miles of railroads in all directions have been at a standstill, and nearly a hundred thousand workmen in voluntary idleness to secure what they regard as justice to their fellow workmen. It has been questioned whether the boycott or strike was wise or whether it was justifiable. On the first question there may be some difference of opinion. It may sincerely be doubted whether it was wise for an organization such as the American Railway Union, within a year of its formation, to attempt to inaugurate a movement which, in its inception, of necessity, assumed gigantic proportions.

The policy or wisdom of entering into so great a movement without consultation with, or against the advice of, the older railroad and *bona-fide* labor organizations of the country is open to serious question. Nor will I attempt from the usual standpoint of trade dispute to justify the strike. Sufficient for me are the facts which provoked it and to which I shall allude later; but that the railroad-men deliberately entered a contest which entailed many sacrifices and dangers in an attempt to redress grievances not of their own, but of other workmen, who, having become thoroughly enervated and impoverished, without organization or previous understanding, in sheer desperation threw down their work, is indeed to their credit.

A little more than twenty years ago George M. Pullman conceived the idea of starting, in connection with his car shops, a town — one that should bear his name and hand down to posterity a monument of his enterprise and philanthropy. He built houses for his employees to live in, stores to make their purchases in, and churches to do their praying in. The workers were told their interests and Mr. Pullman's were one and the same, that what would bring him a greater prosperity would redound to their advantage. They were warned that to belong to a trade-union would be inimical to their *joint* enterprise, hence workmen who would purpose forming a union among them would be discharged, regarded as a common enemy, and driven out of town. They were to depend entirely upon Mr. Pullman's generosity and foresight in all things.

The result was that the workers at Pullman were huddled together in the (outwardly) neat houses, for which they were required to pay higher rents than are paid for similar accommodations in Chicago. They were reduced in wages as often as the seasons would recur and

North American Review, CLIX (August, 1894), 201–206.

opportunities either arose or were made. This was carried on until last February, when a reduction in wages was offered varying from 25 to 33 1/3 and in a few instances 50 per cent.

Here are a few figures which may be taken as a fair criterion of the extent of the reduction in wages offered:

	Price per piece, 1893	Price offered, 1894
Making trolley roofs	$2.25	$1.40
Framework car seat	1.25	.79
Cutting carpets	3.00	1.50
Making mattresses double	.25	.15
Cutting brussels carpet	2.50	1.10
Blacksmith work, platform	4.00	2.65
Truck setting	.45	.16
Sleeping car bodies	180.00	115.50

The workmen being driven to desperation, a meeting was held. Who called it no one knows; how it came about not a vestige of evidence is at hand. It was held and a committee appointed to wait upon Mr. Pullman or a representative of the company, to show that it was absolutely impossible to live on the wages offered; that a middle ground should be sought; that if wages were to be reduced the rents should also come down. Instead of the request of the men being considered by Mr. Pullman, the committee was summarily dismissed and discharged almost instantly. Is it surprising that these men in their rude awakening, finding themselves injured and insulted and their spokesmen discharged and blacklisted, and themselves without an organization to protect or defend them, without the means of properly laying their grievances before organized labor of the country, struck work, declaring that they might as well remain idle and starve as work and slowly meet that fate?

Organized labor of Chicago, becoming aware of the unusual commotion at Pullman, did not hold against the workers of that town their previous refusals to organize. It was readily appreciated that these men had been wholly misled by false promises and covert threats. Relief committees were at once formed, and it is fairly declared that the average workmen of that town have fared better since they engaged in the contest and fraternized with their fellow-workmen than they have for the past two years while working.

It was during this time, when relief committees from the Pullman strikers were making their visits to organizations, that the American Railway Union was holding its first convention in Chicago, and a committee called upon it for its financial and moral assistance. A committee from the convention was appointed to wait upon the company with the request that the matter in dispute might be submitted to arbitration. The committee was told that there was nothing to arbitrate and that the company refused to discuss the matter at all. Insulted, humiliated by the manner in which their disinterested efforts at restoring amicable relations between Mr. Pullman and his former servile employees were received, the committee made its report. The convention in a moment reflected the feelings of the committee, and though at first sullen, silent, and indignant they resolved amidst the wildest enthusiasm that unless the Pullman company either adjusted the matter in controversy with their employees or submitted it to arbitration the members of the American Railway Union would not handle Pullman cars and would ask all workmen to act likewise. No heed was given to the request, resolution, or threat (call it what you will), and the great boycott (strike) was on.

I can scarcely bring myself to the belief that the convention imagined that the movement would be as extended as it became, nor that it would last as long as it did. Be that as it may, we certainly found ourselves in the midst of one of the greatest labor struggles.

Now comes the question repeated: Was the strike wise or justifiable? the answer to which must always depend upon the character and position of the party giving it. As to the wisdom, time only can tell. Since "nothing succeeds so well as success" in all efforts of life, I presume this element will finally set its *quietus* upon this consideration of the subject. But was it justifiable? From the standpoint of the employer, No. From the standpoint of a labor organization having an agreement with an employer whose provisions a strike would violate, No. From the standpoint of the A. R. U., having no agreement with either of the railroad companies involved, and expressing the inarticulate protest of the masses against the wrongs inflicted upon any of their brothers and their yearning for justice to all mankind, Yes; a thousand times yes.

It is something not yet fully understood how thoroughly organized labor stands as the sturdy pioneer of all the hopes of the masses for justice and humane conditions, of their aspirations for a nobler manhood resultant from an equality of opportunities. It is in consequence of these facts that organized labor feels itself frequently called upon to espouse the cause of those who have neglected their own interests, and who have even antagonized any effort to bring them within the fold of organization. Laboring men feel and know that the wealth producers would certainly avail themselves of their only means of defending and advancing their position in life

were it not that they in many instances had their prejudices aroused and their ignorance of actual conditions preyed upon by the instruments of their oppression in the hands of the corporate and employing class. But the men are on strike, the police armed to the teeth are on guard to protect life and property, the militia are called out ostensibly for the same purpose, and the regular army of the United States are marshalled into the fields by order of the President to enforce injunctions, restraining "everybody" from even writing a letter, issued by the Judge who only a few days before expressed the firm conviction that the growth of labor organizations must be checked by law.

Is it not somewhat strange that the provisions of the Interstate Commerce Law, a law passed by Congress in compliance with the demand of the people of our country to protect them against the greed and outrageous discriminations of the railroads, can be distorted to such a degree as to appall its authors and promoters, and should be perverted from its true purpose, and made to do service as an instrument to oppress the parties to whom it was never intended to apply, workingmen engaged in a contest to redress grievances. One may look almost in vain for the restraint the law has put upon the avarice and injustice practised by the railroad corporations. The reform elements in our country seem to have unconsciously created their own Frankenstein, the breath of life being injected into it by plutocracy in the shape of illgotten gains.

There is no desire nor even a tendency on the part of organized labor to have its movement go beyond the limits of the law, but I submit that there is a standpoint from which this great problem should be considered other than a judge's injunction, a policeman's club, or the point of the bayonet. The fact of the matter is that industrial conditions have changed to a wonderful extent within the past thirty years, that wealth has been accumulated as never before, that new forces are at play in the production and transportation of wealth, and that the civil law of our States and country has simply not kept pace in becoming accommodated to the altered conditions. Do what you will, declaim as you may, industrial and commercial development cannot be confined within the limits of laws enacted to fit past decades the theories of which are sought to be applied to modern conditions.

Civilization of the past and present is based upon labor, and yet the laborer has no standing nor protection in the economy of our life. It may well be asked, if the state refuses to deal out some degree of justice and guarantee protection to labor, what interest has the laborer in the state? As a matter of fact the organizations of labor are endeavoring to secure that protection and guaranty to the workingmen which the state has failed to take cognizance of. Without organization the workmen would simply be reduced to a much worse condition than the slaves in antebellum days, and all attempts to strain the law, construing the exercise of natural rights to be criminal, will only react upon the heads of the legal prestidigitators.

If in monarchical England, with its old and effete traditions and crusty customs, Parliament can afford to liberalize its laws and legalize the action of working-men engaged in the maintenance of their organizations and their effort to obtain better conditions, certainly the Republic of these United States should not only keep pace with that spirit, but advance beyond it, and not bring the entire military and civil forces to aid the strong and help crush out the weak.

Labor cannot, and will not if it could, utilize the process of securing legislation by the use of money; it relies upon the justice of its cause, the nobility of its purposes, the humanizing influences of its efforts.

Mr. Pullman, it is said, is willing to spend millions of dollars if necessary to bring his former employees "to their senses." That is to say, he is willing to spend millions of dollars to bring his workmen to the sense of their utter dependence upon him.

This is evidently his purpose. It is the purpose of many another corporation king. He and a few others may possibly win for the present, but the people of America, when once aroused to a sense of the wrong inflicted upon them, will not be slow in so shaping our laws and industrial conditions as to surprise their most supercilious critics.

We insist upon the right to organize, the right to think, to act; to protect ourselves, our homes, and our liberties, and work out our emancipation. We are confident we shall secure them, and that the world will stand surprised that they were accomplished through the means of an enlightened public opinion and by peaceful means.

Wade Hampton: THE LESSON OF THE RECENT STRIKES

THERE can be no possible excuse for conduct such as that which has characterized the acts of the lawless mobs, who, in defiance of all laws, divine and human, blindly and madly struck at the very foundation of all organized society, seemingly only intent on involving the whole country in common ruin. There can be no palliation for outrages such as they have committed, and their conduct has been as senseless as it is inexcusable, for if in their mad rage they bring about a war of labor against capital, there can be but one result to it — a disastrous one to the originators. Should such a fearful conflict occur, the misguided men, who, under the influence of evil counsels, seek to remedy their grievances by unlawful means, would inevitably be the severest sufferers, for not only would all their means of livelihood be swept away, but hundreds, perhaps thousands, of them would lose their lives.

I have said that this strike was inexcusable. The ostensible reason given for it by the strikers is that Mr. Pullman did not pay his employees sufficient wages. In answer to this charge, Mr. Pullman says that he cannot pay more for the manufacture of a car than the price he can obtain for it from the railroads. Every business man must admit that this answer is conclusive and logical. But admitting, for the sake of argument, that his employees were right in their contention, does that justify a resort on their part, not only against him and his property, but against all property, private as well as public? What justification can be offered for the order of the leaders of all the labor organizations in the country, connected in any manner with the railroads, that each member should at once throw up his position as evidence of sympathy with the Pullman employees?

And above all other inexplicable questions suggested by the action of the Pullman employees, what semblance of right had these men, who had voluntarily left their employment, to combine unlawfully with men whose object was the destruction of the railroads and of property of all other descriptions? The workmen of the Pullman company were not connected with railroads in any manner; their sole business was in the construction of sleeping cars, and yet, when they threw up their position, they joined in the work of wrecking the roads, obstructing travel, stopping the mails, and defying the laws of the land. Another strange feature in this matter is the action taken by A. R. U., an organization in no wise connected with the Pullman company but, notwithstanding this fact, this body of railroad employees decreed that no railroad should use Pullman cars! The railroads, many of which were under contract to use these cars, naturally and properly paid no respect to this order emanating as it did from an irresponsible source, whereupon these sympathetic strikers of the A. R. U. became enemies of the public peace, and resorted to violence, robbery, and bloodshed, to enforce their lawless demands. And these things are done on our own soil, where it has been the proud boast that the laws were supreme, guaranteeing to every citizen equal rights! But it seems that the new doctrine announced by the A. R. U. puts the railroads of the country outside of the pale of the law, leaving the vast interests of these corporations, as well as those of

North American Review, CLIX (August, 1894), 190–194.

their bondholders, at the mercy of any mob of ignorant or vicious men. To our shame, too, there are men in high position who uphold these careless proceedings and who defend the perpetrators. We have surely fallen on strange and evil times, and conservative men of all sections and of all parties should devote all efforts to the restoration of order and the maintenance of law. There is not one present vested right of individuals, of corporations, or one of government ownership of property that would be safe if the criminal acts recently committed by riotous mobs in several of the States are permitted to go unpunished. Life itself would no longer be safe, for in more than one instance murder was added to the long list of atrocities which marked the carnival of crime that held mad sway of late in many portions of our country. And the hollow pretence given by those strikers for the outrages they committed is the assertion that they were endeavoring to aid the former workmen of the Pullman company. Every interest of the country is to be sacrificed, every vested right is to be trampled upon, every principle of law and of morals is to be violated, simply because workmen engaged in a particular business cannot obtain the wages they demand. How could these workmen be possibly benefited by the lawless and indiscreet conduct of such misguided sympathizers? No right, no principle, can be established by the commission of a wrong.

For this unholy alliance between unemployed workmen and the disreputable and worst elements of our population to succeed would, indeed, be the consecration of a crime. The President has been criticised, even denounced, because he attempted to prevent the consummation of the crimes contemplated against the peace, the honor, and the welfare of the

country; and the ground upon which this attack on him is based is that his action has been in violation of the rights of States. No one upholds whatever of States' rights is left to us more earnestly than myself, but I can see no force in the charge that the President has, by his course, exceeded the authority conferred on him by the Constitution and the laws made in pursuance of that instrument. Those who hold that the President has, by sending Federal troops to the scenes of disorder, exceeded his power predicate their opinion on Sec. 4, Article 4, of the Constitution, which authorizes Congress to send troops to any State "to protect it against invasion, and, on application of the legislature (or of the executive when the legislature cannot be convened), against domestic violence." The meaning of this provision is perfectly clear. Congress is authorized to send troops to any State on the call of the legislature, or of the governor, under certain conditions, when the authorities of such State are unable to repel invasion or to repress domestic violence. But those who criticise the acts of the President forget that Congress has enacted laws which confer on the chief magistrate larger and wider powers than those given to Congress by the Constitution. The authority for the exercise of those powers is found in Sections 5298 and 5299 of the Revised Statutes. A reference to those laws will prove that the President not only has absolute power to call on the Federal forces to suppress "any insurrection, violence, unlawful combination or conspiracy" occurring in any State, and indeed it is made "his duty to take such measures, by the employment of the militia, or the land and naval force of the United States, or of either, or by other means, as he may deem necessary for the suppression of such insurrection domestic violence or combinations." These quotations from Section 5299 are sufficient to show how ample is the authority of the President to deal with such cases as those confronting him now, and it should be a source of heartfelt congratulation to all law-abiding citizens that the executive chair is now filled by one, who, knowing what his duty demanded of him, had the courage to discharge it promptly, fully, and fearlessly. There is another potent reason why the Federal authorities should have been called on to intervene in suppressing the riots which occurred, and why the shield of Federal authority should have been interposed for the protection of property. The government has millions of dollars invested in the trans-continental railroads, secured by mortgages on these roads, and it was the clear duty of the President to use all the means in his power to guard this immense property from destruction, for the whole country is interested in its preservation. Lawless mobs have not only stopped traffic and travel on these roads, thus cutting off the legitimate revenue due to the Government, but they have in many instances destroyed the roads and burned the bridges on them. If such outrages are permitted to go unpunished, our laws are a farce, for they give protection neither to life nor to property. Every consideration of duty, self-respect, honor, interest, demands that the majesty of the law should be vindicated whatever the cost of doing so may be. Every humane man must feel profound sympathy for all honest toilers where labor does not yield proper remuneration; but no legislation, no government, no earthly power, can rectify the immutable law by which the gifts of fortune are distributed with an unequal hand. It has been so since the beginning of the world and it will probably so continue to the end, or to the millennium, for our Divine Master said, "The poor ye have always with you."

United States Strike Commission: LOSSES AND CRIMES DURING THE PULLMAN DISPUTE

ACCORDING to the testimony the railroads lost in property destroyed, hire of United States deputy marshals, and other incidental expenses, at least $685,308. The loss of earnings of these roads is estimated at $4,672,916. Some 3,100 employees at Pullman lost in wages, as estimated, at least $350,000. About 100,000 employees upon the 24 railroads centering at Chicago, all of which were more or less involved in the strike, lost in wages, as estimated, at least $1,389,143. Many of these employees are still adrift and losing wages.

Beyond these amounts very great losses, widely distributed, were incidentally suffered throughout the country. The suspension of transportation at Chicago paralyzed a vast distributive center, and imposed many hardships and much loss upon the great number of people whose manufacturing and business operations, employment, travel, and necessary supplies depend upon and demand regular transportation service to, from, and through Chicago.

During the strike the fatalities, arrests, indictments, and dismissals of charges for strike offenses in Chicago and vicinity were as follows:

United States Strike Commission, *Report on the Chicago Strike*, June–July, 1894, Senate Executive Document No. 7, 53d Congress, 3d session, pp. xviii–xix.

Number shot and fatally wounded	12
Number arrested by the police	515
Number arrested under United States statutes and against whom indictments were found	71
Number arrested against whom indictments were not found	119

The arrests made by the police were for murder, arson, burglary, assault, intimidation, riot, inciting to riot, and lesser crimes. The cases passed upon by the special United States grand jury, which convened on July 10, 1894, related to obstruction of the mail, forbidden by Section 3995 of the United States Revised Statutes; conspiracy to commit offenses against the United States, forbidden by Section 5440 of the Revised Statutes; conspiracy in restraint of trade or commerce among the several States, forbidden by Chapter 647 of the United States, laws of 1890; conspiracy to injure, oppress, threaten, or intimidate citizens in the free exercise and enjoyment of their rights and privileges under the Constitution and Laws of the United States, forbidden by Section 5508 of the United States Revised Statutes.

Several indictments were found against Eugene V. Debs, George W. Howard, L. W. Rogers, and Sylvester Keliher, officers of the American Railway Union, under these different statutes. Neither indictments nor proceedings were had under the act to regulate commerce, approved February 4, 1887, as has been sometimes stated.

These great losses and many crimes; the vast numbers, strength, and resources of the labor that contended under the leadership of the American Railway Union upon the one side and Pullman's Palace Car Company and the General Managers' Association upon the other; the attitude of labor toward capital, dis-closed in its readiness to strike sympathetically; the determination of capital to crush the strike rather than to accept any peaceable solution through conciliation, arbitration, or otherwise; the certainty with which vast strikes let loose the disreputable to burn, plunder, and even murder; the conversion of industrious and law-abiding men into idlers, lawbreakers, or associates of criminals; the want brought to many innocent families; the transformation of railroad yards, tracks, and stations, as well as the busy marts of trade, into armed camps; the possibilities of future strikes on more extended lines of union against even greater combinations of capital — are all factors bearing upon the present industrial situation which need to be thoroughly understood by the people and to be wisely and prudently treated by the government.

TROOPS, MILITARY, ETC.

For the protection of city, state, and federal property, for the suppression of crime and the preservation of order, the city, county, state, and federal forces were utilized as shown in the following statement:

From July 3 to July 10 the number of United States troops sent to and used in Chicago to protect the United States mail service and federal buildings, and to sustain the execution of the orders of the United States courts was	1,936
Between July 6 and July 11 the State militia was ordered on duty at Chicago and remained so long as needed, to the number of about	4,000
Extra deputy marshals, about	5,000
Extra deputy sheriffs	250
Police force of Chicago	3,000
Total	14,186

THE BACKGROUND OF THE DISPUTE

United States Strike Commission: PULLMAN'S
PALACE CAR COMPANY

THIS is a corporation organized in 1867, with a capital of $1,000,000. It has grown until its present paid-up capital is $36,000,000. Its prosperity has enabled the company for over twenty years to pay 2 per cent quarterly dividends, and, in addition, to lay up a surplus of nearly $25,000,000 of undivided profits. From 1867 to 1871 dividends ranging from 9½ to 12 per cent per annum were paid. For the year ending July 31, 1893, the dividends were $2,520,000, and the wages $7,223,719.51. For the year ending July 31, 1894, the dividends were $2,880,000, and the wages $4,471,701.39.

The business of the company is —

(1) The operation of its cars upon about 125,000 miles of railroad, being about three-fourths of the railway mileage of the country, under contracts similar to that in evidence.

(2) The manufacture and repair of such cars.

(3) The manufacture of cars of all kinds for the general market.

(4) The care and management, as owner and landlord, of the town of Pullman.

In 1880 the company bought 500 acres of land, and upon 300 acres of it built its plant and also a hotel, arcade, churches, athletic grounds, and brick tenements suitable for the use of its employees. The town is well laid out and has a complete sewerage and water system. It is beautified by well-kept open spaces and stretches, flower beds, and lakes. The whole is at all times kept in neat order by the company. The main object was the establishment of a great manufacturing business upon a substantial money-making basis. Efficient workmen were regarded as essential to its success, and it was believed that they could be secured, held in contentment, and improved as such for their own sakes and for the benefit of the company by the accommodations and surroundings that were provided.

The principal church and its parsonage are very attractive structures, but often are not occupied because the rental required to be paid is higher than any church society is willing to pay to obtain the gospel privileges to be thereby secured. In the arcade is a tasteful library of books, carefully selected and cared for by the company. Three dollars per year is charged for its use, and as many as 250 persons a year out of from 4,000 to 5,000 employees and residents have at times, as stated by the capable librarian in charge, availed themselves of its opportunities. It is possible that the air of business strictly maintained there, as elsewhere, and their exclusion from any part in its management prevent more universal and grateful acceptance of its advantages by employees. Men, as a rule, even when employees, prefer independence to paternalism in such matters.

The company provides and pays a

U. S. Strike Commission Report, Senate Executive Document No. 7, 53d Congress, 3d session, pp. xxi–xxiii.

physician and surgeon by the year to furnish to injured employees necessary treatment and drugs. It is, however, also a part of his employment to secure from the injured party a written statement as to the causes of injury, and it is his custom to urge the acceptance of any offered settlement. If suit follows, the doctor is usually a witness for the company. We have no evidence that the doctor has ever abused his confidential relation toward the injured employees; but the system is admirably conceived from a business standpoint to secure speedy settlement of claims for damages upon terms offered by the company and to protect the company from litigation and its results.

Prior to June, 1893, all went well and as designed; the corporation was very prosperous, paid ample and satisfactory wages, as a rule, and charged rents which caused no complaint. During this period those defects in the system which have recently come to the surface and intensified differences, such, for instance, as the refusal to permit the employees to buy land in Pullman and build homes there, caused no disturbance.

As the result of the Pullman system and its growth, when the depression of 1893 came, morally calling for mutual concessions as to wages, rents, etc., we find on the one side a very wealthy and unyielding corporation, and upon the other a multitude of employees of comparatively excellent character and skill, but without local attachments or any interested responsibility in the town, its business, tenements, or surroundings.

The conditions created at Pullman enable the management at all times to assert with great vigor its assumed right to fix wages and rents absolutely, and to repress that sort of independence which leads to labor organizations and their attempts at mediation, arbitration, strikes, etc.

United States Strike Commission: THE AMERICAN RAILWAY UNION

THIS is an association of about 150,000 railroad employees, as alleged, organized at Chicago on the 20th of June, 1893, for the purpose of including railway employees born of white parents in one great brotherhood.

The theory underlying this movement is that the organization of different classes of railroad employees (to the number of about 140,000) upon the trade-union idea has ceased to be useful or adequate; that pride of organization, petty jealousies, and the conflict of views into which men are trained in separate organizations under different leaders, tend to defeat the common object of all, and enable railroads to use such organizations against each other in contentions over wages, etc.; that the rapid concentration of railroad capital and management demands a like union of their employees for the purpose of mutual protection; that the interests of each of the 850,000 and over railroad employees of the United States as to wages, treatment, hours of labor, legislation, insurance, mutual aid, etc., are common to all, and hence all ought to belong to one organization that shall assert its united strength in the protection of the rights of every member.

Excerpted from U. S. Strike Commission Report, Senate Executive Document No. 7, 53d Congress, 3d session, pp. xxiii–xxvii.

In the American Railway Union there are departments of literature and education, legislation, cooperation, mediation, insurance, etc. The organization consists of a general union and of local unions. The general union is formed by representatives of local unions, who elect a board of nine directors quadrennially. This board has authority to "issue such orders and adopt such measures as may be required to carry out the objects of the order." Any ten white persons employed in railway service, except superintendents, etc., can organize a local union. Each local union has its board of mediation, and the chairmen of the various local boards upon a system of railroads constitute a general board of mediation for that system.

In March, 1894, the employees of Pullman's Palace Car Company, being dissatisfied with their wages, rents, and shop treatment for the first time in the history of the town, sought organization, and joined the American Railway Union in large numbers. Their meetings were held outside of Pullman, because the town has no facilities for such purposes.

The Pullman company is hostile to the idea of conferring with organized labor in the settlement of differences arising between it and its employees. . . .

Since the strike, withdrawal from the American Railway Union is required from those seeking work. The company does not recognize that labor organizations have any place or necessity in Pullman, where the company fixes wages and rents, and refuses to treat with labor organizations. The laborer can work or quit on the terms offered; that is the limit of his rights. To join a labor organization in order to secure the protection of union against wrongs, real or imaginary, is over-stepping the limit and arouses hostility. This position secures all the advantage of the concentration of capital, ability, power, and control for the company in its labor dealings, and deprives the employees of any such advantage or protection as a labor union might afford. In this respect the Pullman company is behind the age.

To admit the Pullman shop employees, however, into the American Railway Union as "persons employed in railway service" was not wise or expedient. The constitution can not fairly be construed to include as eligible members those who build cars and run them in and out over private switches. Such loose construction of a labor constitution is certain to involve any organization in such an infinite variety of conflicting positions and to force it into so many contests demanding different and perhaps apparently inconsistent treatment at the same time as to curtail its usefulness and threaten its existence. To reach out and take in those so alien to its natural membership as the Pullman employees, was, in the inception of the organization at least, a mistake. This mistake led the union into a strike purely sympathetic and aided to bring upon it a crushing and demoralizing defeat.

It is undoubtedly true that the officers and directors of the American Railway Union did not want a strike at Pullman, and that they advised against it, but the exaggerated idea of the power of the union, which induced the workmen at Pullman to join the order, led to their striking against this advice. Having struck, the union could do nothing less, upon the theory at its base, than support them.

The union was as yet young; its membership was not as extensive as it hoped to obtain; its workings had the roughness of incipient effort in a new direction; it had recently attained some success in a strike upon the "Great Northern," and had thus aroused extravagant expectations among its members generally; great business depression prevailed; large numbers were idle and stood ready to accept almost any offer of work. For these reasons the officers and directors of the union knew that the times were inopportune for striking and did not advocate it.

A union embracing all railroad employees, even, is as yet a doubtful experiment. Such a union will have great difficulty in moulding itself to the complex character, nationalities, habits, employments, and requirements of its vast and varied membership. . . .

United States Strike Commission: THE GENERAL MANAGERS' ASSOCIATION

THIS voluntary, unincorporated association was formed in 1886, and has as members the 24 railroads centering or terminating in Chicago. The following facts relating to these roads for the year ending June 30, 1894, have been furnished by the Interstate Commerce Commission:

Number of miles operated	40,933
Number of stockholders	52,088
Capitalization:	
Capital stock	$818,569,004
Funded debt	$1,210,235,702
Current liabilities	$79,747,911
Total	$2,108,552,617
Gross earnings	$325,825,726
Net earnings	$102,710,917
Number of employees	221,097

In its constitution the object of the association is stated to be "the consideration of problems of management arising from the operation of railroads terminating or centering at Chicago." It further provides that "all funds needed shall be raised by assessments divided equally among the members." There are no limitations as to "consideration of problems" or "funds" except the will of the managers and the resources of the railroad corporations.

Prior to the recent strike the association was chiefly concerned with matters other than wages. It dealt with all questions concerning transportation centering at Chicago in which the roads had a common interest. It thus determined the policy and practically fixed the relations of all the roads toward the public as to switching, car service, loading and unloading cars, weights of live stock, rates, etc., and sustained each road in maintaining the position of the association as to these matters.

Until June, 1894, the association dealt incidentally and infrequently with wages. There were few railroad controversies as to wages during its active life, dating from January 20, 1892. Hence its possibilities as a strike fighter and wage arbiter lay rather dormant. The following are instances of its action as to wage questions. Its roads fixed a "Chicago scale" for switchmen, covering all lines at Chicago. In March, 1893, the switchmen demanded more pay from each road. The association concluded that they were paid enough — if anything, too much. The roads so informed the men. The Switchmen's Mutual Aid Association of North America wrote to Mr. St. John, as chairman, acquiescing. He, as chairman

Excerpted from U. S. Strike Commission Report, Senate Executive Document No. 7, 53d Congress, 3d session, pp. xxviii–xxxi.

of the General Managers' Association, concluded his reply as follows:

The association approves the course taken by your body and desires to deal fairly with all employees and believes *that our switchmen* are receiving due consideration.

This seems to show that employees upon association roads are treated as under subjection to the General Managers' Association. . . .

This association likewise prepared for its use elaborate schedules of the wages paid upon the entire lines of its 24 members. The proposed object of these schedules was to let each road know what other roads paid. Finding that the men upon some lines urged increases to correspond with wages paid elsewhere, a committee of the association prepared and presented a uniform schedule for all membership roads. It was deemed wise not to act upon the report. It was distributed to members in November, 1893. This distribution alone enabled the report to be used with efficiency as an "equalizer." As the result, during 1893 — it being then well understood that as to wages, etc., it was an *incident* of the General Managers' Association to "assist" each road in case of trouble over such matters, one form of assistance being for the association to secure men enough through its agencies to take the places of all strikers — reductions were here and there made on the different roads, the tendency and effort apparently being to equalize the pay on all lines.

It is admitted that the action of the association has great weight with outside lines, and thus tends to establish one uniform scale throughout the country. The further single step of admitting lines not running into Chicago to membership would certainly have the effect of combining all railroads in wage contentions against all employees thereon.

The commission questions whether any legal authority, statutory or otherwise, can be found to justify some of the features of the association which have come to light in this investigation. If we regard its practical workings rather than its professions as expressed in its constitution, the General Managers' Association has no more standing in law than the old Trunk Line Pool.[1] . . .

It should be noted that until the railroads set the example a general union of railroad employees was never attempted. The unions had not gone beyond enlisting the men upon different systems in separate trade organizations. These neutralize and check each other to some extent and have no such scope or capacity for good or evil as is possible under the universal combination idea inaugurated by the railroads and followed by the American Railway Union. The refusal of the General Managers' Association to recognize and deal with such a combination of labor as the American Railway Union seems arrogant and absurd when we consider its standing before the law, its assumptions, and its past and obviously contemplated future action. . . .

[1] [To restrain competition, which was often of a cut-throat character, railroads had, during the 1870's and 1880's, entered into illegal pools which divided traffic and revenue. ED.]

United States Strike Commission: PULLMAN
COMPANY'S STATEMENT

IN view of the proposed attempt of the American Railway Union to interfere with public travel on railway lines using Pullman cars, in consequence of a controversy as to the wages of employees of the manufacturing department of the company, the Pullman company requests the publication of the following statement of the facts, in face of which the attempt is to be made:

In the first week of May last [1894] there were employed in the car manufacturing department at Pullman, Ill., about 3,100 persons. On May 7, a committee of the workmen had an interview by arrangement with Mr. Wickes, vice-president, at which the principal subject of discussion related to wages, but minor grievances as to shop administration were also presented, and it was agreed that another meeting should be held on the 9th of May, at which all the grievances should be presented in writing. The second meeting was held. As to the complaints on all matters except wages, it was arranged that a formal and thorough investigation should be made by Mr. Wickes, to be begun the next day, and full redress was assured to the committee as to all complaints proved to be well founded.

The absolute necessity of the last reduction in wages, under the existing condition of the business of car manufacturing, had been explained to the committee, and they were insisting upon a restoration of the wage scale of the first half of 1893, when Mr. Pullman entered the room and addressed the committee, speaking in substance as follows:

At the commencement of the very serious depression last year, we were employing at Pullman 5,816 men, and paying out in wages there $305,000 a month. Negotiations with intending purchasers of railway equipment that were then pending for new work were stopped by them, orders already given by others were canceled, and we were obliged to lay off, as you are aware, a large number of men in every department, so that by November 1, 1893, there were only about 2,000 men in all departments, or about one-third of the normal number. I realized the necessity for the most strenuous exertions to procure work immediately, without which there would be great embarrassment, not only to the employees and their families at Pullman, but also to those living in the immediate vicinity, including between 700 and 800 employees who had purchased homes and to whom employment was actually necessary to enable them to complete their payments.

I canvassed the matter thoroughly with the manager of the works and instructed him to cause the men to be assured that the company would do everything in its power to meet the competition which was sure to occur because of the great number of large car manufacturers that were in the same condition, and that were exceedingly anxious to keep their men employed. I knew that if there was any work to be let, bids for it would be made upon a much lower basis than ever before.

The result of this discussion was a revision in piecework prices, which, in the absence of any information to the contrary, I supposed to be acceptable to the men under the circumstances. Under these conditions, and with lower prices upon all materials, I personally undertook the work of the lettings of cars, and by making lower bids than other manufacturers I secured work enough to

U. S. Strike Commission Report, Senate Executive Document No. 7, 53d Congress, 3d session, pp. 578–581.

gradually increase our force from 2,000 up to about 4,200, the number employed, according to the April pay rolls, in all capacities at Pullman.

Says company bears its share

This result has not been accomplished merely by reduction in wages, but the company has borne its full share by eliminating from its estimates the use of capital and machinery, and in many cases going even below that and taking work at considerable loss, notably the 55 Long Island cars, which was the first large order of passenger cars let since the great depression and which was sought for by practically all the leading car builders in the country. My anxiety to secure that order, so as to put as many men at work as possible, was such that I put in a bid at more than $300 per car less than the actual cost to the company. The 300 stock cars built for the Northwestern road and the 250 refrigerator cars now under construction for the same company will result in a loss of at least $12 per car, and the 25 cars just built for the Lake Street elevated road show a loss of $79 per car. I mention these particulars so that you may understand what the company has done for the mutual interests and to secure for the people at Pullman and vicinity the benefit of the disbursement of the large sums of money involved in these and similar contracts, which can be kept up only by the procurement of new orders for cars, for, as you know, about three-fourths of the men must depend upon contract work for employment.

I can only assure you that if this company now restores the wages of the first half of 1893, as you have asked, it would be a most unfortunate thing for the men, because there is less than sixty days of contract work in sight in the shops under all orders and there is absolutely no possibility, in the present condition of affairs throughout the country, of getting any more orders for work at prices measured by the wages of May, 1893. Under such a scale the works would necessarily close down and the great majority of the employees

be put in idleness, a contingency I am using my best efforts to avoid.

To further benefit the people of Pullman and vicinity we concentrated all the work that we could command at that point, by closing our Detroit shops entirely and laying off a large number of men at our other repair shops, and gave to Pullman the repair of all cars that could be taken care of there.

Also, for the further benefit of our people at Pullman we have carried on a large system of internal improvements, having expended nearly $160,000 since August last in work which, under normal conditions, would have been spread over one or two years. The policy would be to continue this class of work to as great an extent as possible, provided, of course, the Pullman men show a proper appreciation of the situation by doing whatever they can to help themselves to tide over the hard times which are so seriously felt in every part of the country.

There has been some complaint made about rents. As to this I would say that the return to this company on the capital invested in the Pullman tenements for the last year and the year before was 3.82 per cent. There are hundreds of tenements in Pullman renting for from $6 to $9 per month, and the tenants are relieved from the usual expenses of exterior cleaning and the removal of garbage, which is done by the company. The average amount collected from employees for gas consumed is about $2 a month. To ascertain the exact amount of water used by tenants, separate from the amount consumed by the works, we have recently put in meters, by which we find that the water consumed by the tenants, if paid for at the rate of 4 cents per 1,000 gallons, in accordance with our original contract with the village of Hyde Park, would amount to about $1,000 a month, almost exactly the rate which we have charged the tenants, this company assuming the expense of pumping. At the increased rate the city is now charging us for water we are paying about $500 a month in excess of the amount charged to the tenants. The present pay rolls at Pullman amount to about $7,000 a day.

On the question of rents, while, as stated above, they make a manifestly inadequate return upon the investment, so that it is clear they are not, in fact, at an arbitrarily high figure, it may be added that it would not be possible in a business sense so to deal with them.

The renting of the dwellings and the employment of workmen at Pullman are in no way tied together. The dwellings and apartments are offered for rent in competition with those of the immediately adjacent towns of Kensington, Roseland, and Gano. They are let alike to Pullman employees and to very many others in no way connected with the company, and, on the other hand, many Pullman employees rent or own their homes in those adjacent towns. The average rental at Pullman is at the rate of $3 per room per month. There are 1,200 tenements, of varying numbers of rooms, the average monthly rental of which is $10; of these there are 600 the average monthly rental of which is $8. In very many cases men with families pay a rent seemingly large for a workman, but which is in fact reduced in part, and often wholly repaid, by the subrents paid by single men as lodgers.

Why the shops shut down

On May 10, the day after the second conference above mentioned, work went on at Pullman as usual, and the only incident of note was the beginning by Mr. Wickes, assisted by Mr. Brown, the general manager of the company, of the promised formal investigation at Pullman of the shop complaints.

A large meeting of employees had been held the night before at Kensington, which, as was understood by the company, accepted the necessity of the situation preventing an increase of wages; but at a meeting of the local committee held during the night of May 10 a strike was decided upon, and accordingly the next day about 2,500 of the employees quit their work, leaving about 600 at work, of whom very few were skilled workmen. As it was found impracticable to keep the shops in operation with a force thus diminished and disorganized, the next day those remaining were necessarily laid off, and no work has since been done in the shops.

The payrolls at the time amounted to about $7,000 a day, and were reduced $5,500 by the strike, so that during the period of a little more than six weeks which has elapsed the employees who quit their work have deprived themselves and their comrades of earnings of more than $200,000.

It is an element of the whole situation worthy of note that at the beginning of the strike the Pullman Savings Bank had on deposit in its savings department $488,000, of which about nine-tenths belonged to employees at Pullman, and that this amount has since been reduced by the sum of $32,000.

While deploring the possibility of annoyance to the public by the threats of irresponsible organizations to interrupt the orderly ministration to the comfort of travelers on railway lines, aggregating 125,000 miles in length, the Pullman company can do no more than explain its situation to the public. It has two separate branches of business, essentially distinct from each other. One is to provide sleeping cars, which are delivered by it under contract to the various railway companies, to be run by them on their lines as a part of their trains for the carriage of their passengers, over the movements of which this company has no control. Contract arrangements provide for the making of all repairs to such cars by the railway companies using them — as to certain repairs absolutely, and as to all others upon the request of the Pullman company, which ordinarily finds it most convenient to use its own manufacturing facilities to make such repairs. The other, and a distinct branch of the business of the Pullman company, is the manufacture of sleeping cars for the above-mentioned use of railway companies and the manufacture for sale to railway companies of freight cars and ordinary passenger cars, and of street cars, and this business is almost at a standstill throughout the United States.

The business of manufacturing cars for sale gives employment to about 70 per cent of the shop employees. The manufacture of sleeping cars for use by railway companies under contract, and which, under normal conditions, gives employment to about 15 per cent of the shop employees, can not be resumed by the company to an important extent for a very long time, for out of the provision made for the abnormal travel last year the company now has about 400 sleeping cars in store ready for use, but for which there is no need in the existing conditions of public travel.

It is now threatened by the American Railway Union officials that railway companies using Pullman sleeping cars shall be compelled to deprive their passengers of sleeping-car accommodations, unless the Pullman company will agree to submit to arbitration the question as to whether or not it shall open its manufacturing shops at Pullman and operate them under a scale of wages which would cause a daily loss to it of one-fourth the wages paid. . . .

United States Strike Commission: STATEMENT FROM THE PULLMAN STRIKERS TO THE CONVENTION OF THE AMERICAN RAILWAY UNION
[JUNE 15, 1894]

MR. President and Brothers of the American Railway Union: We struck at Pullman because we were without hope. We joined the American Railway Union because it gave us a glimmer of hope. Twenty thousand souls, men, women, and little ones, have their eyes turned toward this convention to-day, straining eagerly through dark despondency for a glimmer of the heaven-sent message you alone can give us on this earth.

In stating to this body our grievances it is hard to tell where to begin. You all must know that the proximate cause of our strike was the discharge of two members of our grievance committee the day after George M. Pullman, himself, and Thomas H. Wickes, his second vice-president, had guaranteed them absolute immunity. The more remote causes are still imminent. Five reductions in wages, in work, and in conditions of employment swept through the shops at Pullman between May and December, 1893. The last was the most severe, amounting to nearly 30 per cent, and our rents had not fallen. We owed Pullman $70,000 when we struck May 11. We owe him twice as much to-day. He does not evict us for

U. S. Strike Commission Report, Senate Executive Document No. 7, 53d Congress, 3d session, pp. 87–91.

two reasons: One, the force of popular sentiment and public opinion; the other because he hopes to starve us out, to break through in the back of the American Railway Union, and to deduct from our miserable wages when we are forced to return to him the last dollar we owe him for the occupancy of his houses.

Rents all over the city in every quarter of its vast extent have fallen, in some cases to one-half. Residences, compared with which ours are hovels, can be had a few miles away at the prices we have been contributing to make a millionaire a billionaire. What we pay $15 for in Pullman is leased for $8 in Roseland; and remember that just as no man or woman of our 4,000 toilers has ever felt the friendly pressure of George M. Pullman's hand, so no man or woman of us all has ever owned or can ever hope to own one inch of George M. Pullman's land. Why, even the very streets are his. His ground has never been platted of record, and to-day he may debar any man who has acquiring rights as his tenant from walking in his highways. And those streets; do you know what he has named them? He says after the four great inventors in methods of transportation. And do you know what their names are? Why, Fulton, Stephenson, Watt, and Pullman.

Water which Pullman buys from the city at 8 cents a thousand gallons he retails to us at 500 per cent advance and claims he is losing $400 a month on it. Gas which sells at 75 cents per thousand feet in Hyde Park, just north of us, sells for $2.25. When we went to tell him our grievances he said we were all his "children."

Pullman, both the man and the town, is an ulcer on the body politic. He owns the houses, the schoolhouses, and churches of God in the town he gave his once humble name. The revenue he derives from these, the wages he pays out with one hand — the Pullman Palace Car Company, he takes back with the other — the Pullman Land Association. He is able by this to bid under any contract car shop in this country. His competitors in business, to meet this, must reduce the wages of their men. This gives him the excuse to reduce ours to conform to the market. His business rivals must in turn scale down; so must he. And thus the merry war — the dance of skeletons bathed in human tears — goes on, and it will go on, brothers, forever, unless you, the American Railway Union, stop it; end it; crush it out.

Our town is beautiful. In all these thirteen years no word of scandal has arisen against one of our women, young or old. What city of 20,000 persons can show the like? Since our strike, the arrests, which used to average four or five a day, had dwindled down to less than one a week. We are peaceable; we are orderly, and but for the kindly beneficence of kindly-hearted people in and about Chicago we would be starving. We are not desperate to-day, because we are not hungry, and our wives and children are not begging for bread. But George M. Pullman, who ran away from the public opinion that has arisen against him, like the genii from the battle in the Arabian Nights, is not feeding us. He is patiently seated beside his millions waiting for what? To see us starve. We have grown better acquainted with the American Railway Union these convention days, and as we have heard sentiments of the noblest philanthropy fall from the lips of our general officers — your officers and ours — we have learned that there is a balm for all our troubles, and that the box containing it is in your hands to-day only awaiting opening to disseminate its sweet savor of hope.

George M. Pullman, you know, has cut our wages from 30 to 70 per cent. George M. Pullman has caused to be paid in the last year the regular quarterly dividend of 2 per cent on his stock and an extra slice of 1½ per cent, making 9½ per cent on $30,000,000 of capital. George M. Pullman, you know, took three contracts on which he lost less than $5,000. Because he loved us? No. Because it was cheaper to lose a little money in his freight car and his coach shops than to let his workingmen go, but that petty loss, more than made up by us from money we needed to clothe our wives and little ones, was his excuse for effecting a gigantic reduction of wages in every department of his great works, of cutting men and boys and girls with equal zeal, including everyone in the repair shops of the Pullman Palace cars on which such preposterous profits have been made.

George M. Pullman will tell you, if you could go to him to-day, that he was paying better wages than any other car shops in the land. George M. Pullman might better save his breath. We have worked too often beside graduates from other establishments not to know that work for work and skill for skill, no one can compete with us at wages paid for work well done. If his wage list showed a trifle higher, our efficiency still left us heavily the loser. He does not figure on our brain and muscle. He makes his paltry computation in dollars and cents. We will make you proud of us, brothers, if you will give us the hand we need. Help us make our country better and more wholesome. Pull us out of our slough of despond. Teach arrogant grinders of the faces of the poor that there is still a God in Israel, and if need be a Jehovah — a God of battles. Do this, and on that last great day you will stand, as we hope to stand, before the great white throne "like gentlemen unafraid. . . ."

United States Strike Commission: THE PULLMAN STRIKE: ITS CAUSES AND EVENTS

PULLMAN'S Palace Car Company is in the market at all times to obtain all possible contracts to build cars. Its relations with railroads, its large capital and surplus, its complete and well-located plant and efficient management enable it at all times to meet all competitors on at least equal terms. . . .

The depression of 1893 naturally affected the business at once, and to a greater extent in some departments than in others. Matters grew worse until, in the fall of 1893, the company closed its Detroit shops, employing about 800, and concentrated its contract and repair business at Pullman. The company and the railroads had a surplus of cars for the decreased traffic obtainable, and hence pending orders were canceled and car building stopped, except as occasional straggling contracts were obtained at prices which averaged less than shop cost, exclusive of interest upon capital or any charge for depreciation of plant or machinery. . . .

The cut in wages during this period [ED. September 1893–May 1894] averaged about 25 per cent. . . .

During all of this reduction and its attendant suffering none of the salaries of

Excerpted from U. S. Strike Commission Report, Senate Executive Document No. 7, 53d Congress, 3d session, pp. xxxii–xxxix.

the officers, managers, or superintendents were reduced. . . .

In its statements to the public, which are in evidence, the company represents that its object in all it did was to continue operations for the benefit of its workmen and of trades people in and about Pullman and to save the public from the annoyance of interrupted travel. The commission thinks that the evidence shows that it sought to keep running mainly for its own benefit as a manufacturer, that its plant might not rust, that its competitors might not invade its territory, that it might keep its cars in repair, that it might be ready for resumption when business revived with a live plant and competent help, and that its revenue from its tenements might continue.

RENTS

If we exclude the aesthetic and sanitary features at Pullman, the rents there are from 20 to 25 per cent higher than rents in Chicago or surrounding towns for similar accommodations. The aesthetic features are admired by visitors, but have little money value to employees, especially when they lack bread. The company aims to secure 6 per cent upon the cost of its tenements, which cost includes a proportionate share for paving, sewerage, water, parks, etc. It claims now to receive less than 4 per cent. . . .

The company's claim that the workmen need not hire its tenements and can live elsewhere if they choose is not entirely tenable. The fear of losing work keeps them in Pullman as long as there are tenements unoccupied, because the company is supposed, as a matter of business, to give a preference to its tenants when work is slack. . . . While reducing wages the company made no reduction in rents. Its position is that the two matters are distinct, and that none of the reasons

urged as justifying wage reduction by it as an employer can be considered by the company as a landlord.

The company claims that it is simply legitimate business to use its position and resources to hire in the labor market as cheaply as possible and at the same time to keep rents up regardless of what wages are paid to its tenants or what similar tenements rent for elsewhere; to avail itself to the full extent of business depression and competition in reducing wages, and to disregard these same conditions as to rents. No valid reason is assigned for this position except simply that the company had the power and the legal right to do it. . . .

THE STRIKE

The reductions at Pullman after September, 1893, were the result of conferences among the managers; the employees for the first time knew of them when they took effect. No explanations or conferences took place until May 7 and 9 in regard thereto between the employees and the officers of the company. For the reasons stated the employees at Pullman were during the winter in a state of chronic discontent. Upon May 7 and 9 a committee of 46 from all the departments waited upon the management and urged the restoration of wages to the basis of June, 1893. The company refused this, and offered no concession as to wages whatever, maintaining and explaining that business conditions did not justify any change. The company based its entire contention as to every department upon the facts in reference to car building to which we have alluded, and offered to show its books and figures as to the cost and selling prices of cars. This offer, on account of the strike intervening, was not acted upon. Had it been, it would have resulted in the figures we have noted as to car-building contracts. The purpose of the management was obviously to rest the whole matter upon cost, etc., in its most seriously crippled department, excluding from consideration the facts as to wages in the repair department, to which we have alluded.

The demand of the employees for the wages of June, 1893, was clearly unjustifiable. The business in May, 1894, could not pay the wages of June, 1893. Reduction was carried to excess, but the company was hardly more at fault therein than were the employees in insisting upon the wages of June, 1893. There was little discussion as to rents, the company maintaining that its rents had nothing to do with its wages and that its revenue from its tenements was no greater than it ought to receive. . . .

The company had a legal right to take this position, but as between man and man the demand for some rent reduction was fair and reasonable under all the circumstances. Some slight concession in this regard would probably have averted the strike, provided the promise not to discharge men who served upon the committee had ·been more strictly regarded.

The next day, May 10, three of the committee were laid off by foremen for alleged lack of work, not an unusual proceeding. Those who made the promise had nothing to do with this action and deny knowledge of it at the time. The foremen who did it are suspected by the employees of concluding that some laying off of committeemen just at that crisis would have a good effect and would accord with the policy and general views of the company. The foremen, however, deny this. This incident was inopportune and unfortunate, to say the least, and ought to have been more carefully guarded against by the company. An explanation of this occurrence was not asked for by the employees, as it ought to have been, before striking.

On the evening of May 10 the local unions met and voted to strike at once. The strike occurred on May 11, and from that time until the soldiers went to Pullman, about July 4, three hundred strikers were placed about the company's property professedly to guard it from destruction or interference. This guarding of property in strikes is, as a rule, a mere pretense. Too often the real object of guards is to prevent newcomers from taking strikers' places, by persuasion, often to be followed, if ineffectual, by intimidation and violence. The Pullman company claims this was the real object of these guards. The strikers at Pullman are entitled to be believed to the contrary in this matter, because of their conduct and forbearance after May 11. It is in evidence, and uncontradicted, that no violence or destruction of property by strikers or sympathizers took place at Pullman, and that until July 3 no extraordinary protection was had from the police or military against even anticipated disorder.

Such dignified, manly, and conservative conduct in the midst of excitement and threatened starvation is worthy of the highest type of American citizenship, and with like prudence in all other directions will result in due time in the lawful and orderly redress of labor wrongs. To deny this is to forswear patriotism and to declare this Government and its people a failure.

As soon as the strike was declared the company laid off its 600 employees who did not join the strike, and kept its shops closed until August 2. During this period the Civic Federation of Chicago, composed of eminent citizens in all kinds of business and from all grades of respectable society, called upon the company twice to urge conciliation and arbitration. The company reiterated the statement of its position, and maintained that there was nothing to arbitrate; that the questions at issue were matters of fact and not proper subjects of arbitration. The Civic Federation suggested that competition should be regarded in rents as well as in wages. The company denied this. Wages and rents were to it separate matters; the principles applicable to one had no relation to the other. Later it gave the same answer to a committee of its employees. Upon June 15 and 22 it declined to receive any communication from committees of the American Railway Union, one proposition of that body being that the company select two arbitrators, the court two, and these four a fifth, to determine whether there was anything to arbitrate. The company also refused to consider any arbitration at the solicitation of the common council of Chicago, and repeated its stereotyped answer that there was nothing to arbitrate when appealed to by Mayor Pingree, of Detroit, himself a large manufacturer, whom Mayor Hopkins accompanied to Pullman. At that interview Mayor Pingree claimed to have telegrams from the mayors of over fifty of the largest cities, urging that there should be arbitration.

THE RAILWAY BOYCOTT:
SUMMARY OF EVENTS

United States Strike Commission: SUMMARY OF THE BOYCOTT

BETWEEN June 9 and June 26 [1894] a regular convention of the American Railway Union was held with open doors at Chicago, representing 465 local unions and about 150,000 members, as claimed. The Pullman matter was publicly discussed at these meetings before and after its committees above mentioned reported their interviews with the Pullman company. On June 21 the delegates, under instructions from their local unions, unanimously voted that the members of the union should stop handling Pullman cars on June 26 unless the Pullman company would consent to arbitration. On June 26 the boycott and strike began. The strike on the part of the railroad employees was a sympathetic one. No grievances against the railroads had been presented by their employees, nor did the American Railway Union declare any such grievances to be any cause whatever of the strike. To simply boycott Pullman cars would have been an incongruous step for the remedy of complaints of railroad employees. Throughout the strike the strife was simply over handling Pullman cars, the men being ready to do their duty otherwise. The contracts between the railroads and the Pullman company as to Pullman cars created such close relations between them as to increase the natural sympathy of organization between the members of the American Railway Union upon railroads and their brothers at Pullman. It is also apparent that the readiness to strike sympathetically was promoted by the disturbed and apprehensive condition of railroad employees resulting from wage reductions on different lines, blacklisting, etc., and from the recent growth and development of the General Managers' Association, which seemed to them a menace. Hence the railroad employees were ripe to espouse the cause of the Pullman strikers. In some instances they struck in disregard of existing contracts between their different organizations and the railroads, notably upon the Illinois Central. They evaded the responsibility of their organizations for this conduct by claiming to act as individuals. They justified themselves under the idea of balancing wrongs.

After June 26 the officers and agents of the union managed and urged on the strike at every available point upon the railroads centering at Chicago until it reached proportions far in excess of their original anticipations, and led to disorders beyond even their control. Urgent solicitations and appeals to strike and to stand firm continued in the many public meetings held each day in and about Chicago, and appeared in the telegrams sent about the country.

On July 7 the principal officers of the

Excerpted from U. S. Strike Commission Report, Senate Executive Document No. 7, 53d Congress, 3d session, pp. xxxix–xlvi.

American Railway Union were indicted, arrested, and held under $10,000 bail. Upon July 13 they were attached for contempt of the United States court in disobeying an injunction issued on July 2 and served on the 3d and 4th, enjoining them, among other things, from compelling, or inducing by threats, intimidation, persuasion, force, or violence, railroad employees to refuse or fail to perform their duties. It is seriously questioned, and with much force, whether courts have jurisdiction to enjoin citizens from "persuading" each other in industrial or other matters of common interest. However, it is generally recognized among good citizens that a mandate of a court is to be obeyed until it is modified and corrected by the court that issued it.

ACTION OF FEDERATED UNIONS

Upon July 12, at the request of the American Railway Union, about 25 of the executive officers of national and international labor unions affiliated with the American Federation of Labor met at Chicago. The situation was laid before them. The conference concluded that the strike was then lost; that a general sympathetic strike throughout the country would be unwise and inexpedient, and, at the time, against the best interests of labor. This conference issued a strong and temperate address to members, expressing sympathy with the purposes of the American Railway Union, advising those on strike to return to work, and urging that labor organize more generally, combine more closely, and seek the correction of industrial evils at the ballot box. To some extent the trade unions of Chicago had struck in sympathy, but this movement was checked by the action of the conference of the 12th and extended no further. This action indicates clearer views by labor as to its responsibilities,

the futility of strikes, and the appropriate remedies in this country for labor wrongs.

Upon July 13 the American Railway Union, through the mayor of Chicago, sent a communication to the General Managers' Association offering to declare the strike off, provided the men should be restored to their former positions without prejudice, except in cases where they had been convicted of crime. The General Managers' Association in advance advertised that it would receive no communication whatever from the American Railway Union, and when received returned it unanswered. . . .

At this date, July 13, and for some days previous, the strikers had been virtually beaten. The action of the courts deprived the American Railway Union of leadership, enabled the General Managers' Association to disintegrate its forces, and to make inroads into its ranks. The mobs had worn out their fury, or had succumbed to the combined forces of the police, the United States troops and marshals, and the State militia. The railroads were gradually repairing damages and resuming traffic with the aid of new men and with some of those strikers who had not been offensively active or whose action was laid to intimidation and fear. At this juncture the refusal of the General Managers' Association to treat with the American Railway Union was certainly not conciliatory; it was not unnatural, however, because the association charged the American Railway Union with having inaugurated an unjustifiable strike, laid at its door the responsibilty for all the disorder and destruction that had occurred, and, as the victor in the fight, desired that the lesson taught to labor by its defeat should be well learned.

The policy of both the Pullman company and the Railway Managers' Association in reference to applications to arbitrate closed the door to all attempts at conciliation and settlement of differences. The commission is impressed with the belief, by the evidence and by the attendant circumstances as disclosed, that a different policy would have prevented the loss of life and great loss of property and wages occasioned by the strike. . . .

From June 22 until the practical end of the strike the General Managers' Association directed and controlled the contest on the part of the railroads, using the combined resources of all the roads to support the contentions and insure the protection of each. . . .

The military and police confined themselves to their duty of arresting criminals, dispersing mobs, and guarding property. United States deputy marshals, to the number of 3,600, were selected by and appointed at request of the General Managers' Association, and of its railroads. They were armed and paid by the railroads, and acted in the double capacity of railroad employees and United States officers. While operating the railroads they assumed and exercised unrestricted United States authority when so ordered by their employers, or whenever they regarded it as necessary. They were not under the direct control of any Government official while exercising authority. This is placing officers of the government under control of a combination of railroads. It is a bad precedent, that might well lead to serious consequences.

There is no evidence before the commission that the officers of the American Railway Union at any time participated in or advised intimidation, violence, or destruction of property. They knew and fully appreciated that as soon as mobs ruled, the organized forces of society would crush the mobs and all responsible for them in the remotest degree, and that

this meant defeat. The attacks upon corporations and monopolies by the leaders in their speeches are similar to those to be found in the magazines and industrial works of the day. . . .

. . . From this testimony it is fair to conclude that strikers were concerned in the outrages against law and order, although the number was undoubtedly small as compared with the whole number out. The strikers' experience and training were to be seen in the spiking and misplacing of switches, removing rails, crippling of interlocking systems, the detaching, side tracking, and derailing of cars and engines, placing of coupling pins in engine machinery, blockading tracks with cars, and attempts to detach and run in mail cars. The commission is of the opinion that offenses of this character, as well as considerable threatening and intimidation of those taking strikers' places, were committed or instigated by strikers.

The mobs that took possession of railroad yards, tracks, and crossings after July 3, and that stoned, tipped over, burned, and destroyed cars and stole their contents, were, by general concurrence in the testimony, composed generally of hoodlums, women, a low class of foreigners, and recruits from the criminal classes. Few strikers were recognized or arrested in these mobs, which were without leadership, and seemed simply bent upon plunder and destruction. They gathered wherever opportunity offered for their dastardly work, and, as a rule, broke and melted away when force faced them. In the view that this railroad strike was wrong; that such mobs are well known to be incidental to strikes, and are thereby given an excuse and incentive to gather and to commit crime, the responsibility rests largely with the American Railway Union; otherwise that association, its leaders, and a very large majority of the railroad men on strike are not shown to have had any connection therewith. Labor advocates contend that strikes are the last resort; that they are the industrial war measures of labor to assert and obtain the rights which humanity, morality, and changed conditions demand; that labor can not otherwise arouse interest in its demands, and that, hence, labor is no more responsible for the public disorders and calamities that attend strikes than are the employers who provoke them. Many impartial observers are reaching the view that much of the real responsibility for these disorders rests with the people themselves and with the Government for not adequately controlling monopolies and corporations, and for failing to reasonably protect the rights of labor and redress its wrongs. None assert that laws can completely remedy contentions as to wages, etc., but many do insist that something substantial can be accomplished in this direction if attempted honestly, reasonably, and in good faith.

Ray Ginger: THE RAILWAY STRIKE

THE boycott began slowly. In spite of the convention orders, each ARU lodge was constitutionally forced to hold its own vote to determine whether it would support the boycott. Every lodge voted to enforce the convention's decision. The boycott was not called solely from sympathy with the Pullman workers; the railroad employees were also suffering from blacklists, short hours, wage cuts, discrimination. Also the feeling was widespread that, if the corporations succeeded in conquering the unorganized workers, they would next move against the organized men. Even among skilled workers there was agreement with Debs' statement: "Every concession the railway companies have ever made, has been wrung from them by the power of organized effort." As lodge after lodge voted to quit work, Debs sent them all the same instructions: Use no violence. Stop no trains. Elect a strike committee and send me the name of the chairman. In this way he hoped to keep control over the entire boycott.

By June 27 only five thousand men had left their jobs, but fifteen railroads were tied up. The Managers opened offices in Pittsburgh, Cleveland, Philadelphia, New York, and Buffalo, to recruit strikebreakers; they also opened a central publicity office in Chicago to furnish information to the newspapers. Soon the commercial press raised the cry of "Anarchy"; this charge was doubly effective because President Sadi Carnot of France had been assassinated by an anarchist just two days before the boycott began. The third day, more than forty thousand men had quit work. Traffic was stopped dead on all lines west of Chicago. In spite of Debs' orders to move mail trains, the Postal authorities reported that mails were obstructed at Chicago, St. Paul, and on the Southern Pacific in the Far West. United States Attorneys were instructed by the Justice Department to ask for warrants against all offenders.

One day later, nearly a hundred twenty-five thousand men had joined the boycott. Twenty roads were tied up. A

Ray Ginger, *The Bending Cross: A Biography of Eugene Victor Debs* (New Brunswick, N. J.: Rutgers University Press, 1949), pp. 122–131 excerpted. Used by permission of the publisher.

crowd of a thousand strikers and sympathizers stopped a train on the Chicago & Erie at Hammond, Indiana, and forced the crew to detach two Pullmans. The head of the Switchmen warned that any member of his union supporting the strike would be subject to expulsion, and the Conductor's chief attacked the boycott in the public press.

But several unions rallied to the ARU. J. R. Sovereign pledged aid from the Knights of Labor. The Chicago Federation of Labor, with one hundred fifty thousand members, offered to call a citywide general strike to enforce the boycott. In view of the probable effects on public opinion, Debs refused to sanction such an extreme measure at that stage. . . .

Throughout the East, the Managers continued to hire strikebreakers, and the depression provided hordes of recruits. Intimate grudges also motivated many railroaders to become scabs. One group in New York City told a reporter: "We are going to settle an old account. We were strikers on the Gould roads under Martin Irons [1886], and we haven't handled a switch since then. The men who are striking now are the men who helped to fill our places then. Now we are going west to take their jobs." The Managers easily hired from one hundred to two hundred fifty men daily; by the strike's end nearly twenty-five hundred strikebreakers had been sent to Chicago.

On June 30, in spite of Debs' orders to the contrary, minor violence again occurred. Crowds in Chicago temporarily halted two express trains on the Illinois Central and Panhandle lines. Union leaders were arrested in Indiana and Missouri. The first demand for militia in Illinois came from the Illinois Central, which claimed that its property in Cairo was endangered. Under the laws of Illinois, the governor could call out state troops when the legislature was not in session, but only at the request of the mayor or sheriff. As soon as he had secured permission from these local authorities, Governor Altgeld sent three companies of militia to Cairo. Thomas Milchrist, the Federal district attorney in Chicago, telegraphed to Washington that strikers had stopped mail trains in the suburbs the previous night. He also reported that conditions in Chicago were so bad that special deputies were needed, and recommended that the United States marshal in Chicago be empowered to hire such deputies. This wire by Milchrist exaggerated the actual situation. Five days after he sent the telegram, total strike damages were still less than six thousand dollars. There had been no major riots. The trains halted on the Chicago & Erie, Illinois Central, and Panhandle had soon been allowed to proceed. The telegram from Milchrist was contradicted by a simultaneous telegram from the Superintendent of Railway Mail Service in Chicago, telling the Postmaster General that no mail had accumulated in the city.

Most important of all, the local authorities were confident of their ability to handle the situation. Mayor Hopkins had not even applied to the governor for help, although Altgeld had shown both his willingness and efficiency in controlling labor violence. . . .

The newspaper campaign against the boycott was in full swing, with the Chicago *Tribune* leading the onslaught. On June 30 the *Tribune* let fly with both barrels. One headline read, "Mob Is In Control"; another charged, "Law Is Trampled On"; a third story began: "Through the lawless acts of Dictator Debs' strikers the lives of thousands of Chicago citizens were endangered yesterday." The Chicago *Herald* editorialized: "The necessity is on the railroads to defeat the strike. If they yield one point it will show fatal weakness. If the strike should be successful the owners of the railroad property . . . would have to surrender its future control to the class of labor agitators and strike conspirators who have formed the Debs Railway Union." There were recurrent charges in the press that Debs was a dictator, that he was personally profiting from the strike, that he had called the strike without consulting the union membership. It was widely, and falsely, reported that Debs had ridden in a Pullman car from Chicago to Terre Haute during the boycott.

Immediately after Milchrist sent his telegram to Washington, the General Managers' Association met in closed session at the Rookery Building in Chicago. All newspaper reporters were excluded. At this meeting the railroads agreed that they would not rehire any of the strikers. They also sent a wire to Richard Olney, suggesting that he appoint Edwin Walker as special Federal attorney to handle the strike situation. Walker was, at that time, attorney in Illinois for the Chicago, Milwaukee & St. Paul Railroad, a job he had held since 1870. This railroad was involved in the strike, and was a member of the Managers' Association. A few days earlier, Walker had been asked to handle all strike cases for the railroads. But within two hours, without even pausing to consult Milchrist, Olney had appointed Walker to represent the Federal government. . . .

Opposition to the boycott was gathering intensity. The railroads began deliberately to disrupt their schedules, hoping that the resultant inconvenience to the public would force government intervention. Pullmans were attached to trains that did not customarily carry them — freights, suburbans, and, most

important of all, mail trains, trying to force the strikers to halt the mails. The Brotherhoods accelerated their campaign against the ARU. . . .

Never before had there been such a strike in the United States. More than a hundred thousand men had voluntarily quit work. Between Chicago and the Golden Gate, only the Great Northern was maintaining a semblance of its regular schedule. Everybody in the country had taken sides in the dispute. Debs clearly stated the situation in a speech to the railroaders:

The struggle with the Pullman Company has developed into a contest between the producing classes and the money power of the country. . . . The fight was between the American Railway Union and the Pullman Company. . . . Then the railway corporations, through the General Managers' Association, came to the rescue, and in a series of whereases declared to the world that they would go into partnership with Pullman, so to speak, and stand by him in his devilish work of starving his employees to death.

On July 1, the union was firm at every point, and there was "no sign of violence or disorder," as Debs said. He later claimed that the railroads were losing a fortune daily: "Their immediate resources were exhausted, their properties were paralyzed, and they were unable to operate their trains." Although the ARU had few members in the East and South, it seemed that the boycott might spread to northern New York and perhaps to Pennsylvania. The Central Labor Union of New York City endorsed the boycott, and urged people not to ride in Pullmans until the company accepted arbitration. The Central Labor Union of Chicago took similar action. In spite of the massed billions of Pullman and the railroads, in spite of the newspaper barrage, in spite of strikebreaking by the Brotherhoods and inaction by the AFL, Eugene Debs saw the road to victory stretching bright and certain into the future.

Debs' confidence reckoned without one possibility — Federal intervention. Throughout the critical period of the boycott, President Cleveland was occupied in a bitter fight with Congress over the Wilson Tariff Bill, and his only information about the strike came from Attorney-General Olney.

Richard Olney, from 1859 until his elevation to the cabinet in 1893, had been a corporation lawyer in Boston, representing mainly railroad interests and trust estates. He had also been a director of several railroads: the Eastern, the Boston & Maine, lesser New England lines, the Kansas City & Fort Scott, the Atchinson. Since 1889 he had served on the board of the Burlington, which was involved in the Pullman dispute. His very appearance indicated his dominant characteristics — a narrow honesty, truculence, and stubbornness. . . .

. . . As soon as the Debs Rebellion started, the Attorney-General launched a series of maneuvers to defeat it. He thought that a nation-wide boycott was so essentially violent that Debs' order for peaceful conduct was a mere sham. In a memorandum about the Pullman affair, Olney later wrote: "The President might have used the United States Army to prevent interference with the mails and with interstate commerce on his own initiative — without waiting for action by the courts . . . But . . . it is doubtful . . . whether the President could be induced to move except in support of the judicial tribunals." So the Attorney-General decided to prod Cleveland by securing an injunction against the strike, and then use the Army to enforce the court order. This plan, as well as Olney's intention of

smashing the boycott, was revealed in his telegram to Edwin Walker on June 30: "It has seemed to me that if the rights of the United States were vigorously asserted in Chicago, the origin and centre of the demonstration, the result would be to make it a failure everywhere else and to prevent its spread over the entire country. . . . I feel that the true way of dealing with the matter is by a force which is overwhelming and prevents any attempt at resistance."

Olney's attitude rested on three premises: (1) Any national railroad strike is automatically illegal; (2) The causes of the strike in Pullman were not relevant to the legality of the boycott; (3) The state and local officials could not be trusted to enforce the law. Altgeld, after all, had pardoned the Haymarket survivors, and Mayor Hopkins of Chicago had openly contributed to the relief fund at Pullman. Olney later claimed that Hopkins "even went so far as to openly wear the distinctive badge of the rioters" — a white ribbon was the emblem of the strikers, and Olney thought all strikers were "rioters" in this instance.

In accord with this interpretation, the Attorney-General was trying to persuade the President that the Army should be used at Chicago, and the troops at Fort Sheridan, Illinois, were ordered to hold themselves in readiness. Meanwhile a constant demand for the maintenance of law and order was emanating from the pulpits and the commercial newspapers. On July 2 a headline on the Chicago *Tribune* screeched:

STRIKE IS NOW WAR

And the lead editorial had a shrewd caption:

Six Days Shalt Thou Labor — BIBLE
Not Unless I Say So   — DEBS

That same day, in a crushing blow, Judges Peter Grosscup and William A. Woods of the Federal Court in Chicago issued an omnibus injunction against the ARU leaders. The previous Decoration Day, Judge Grosscup had said in a speech: "The growth of labor organizations must be checked by law." It was later shown that Judge Woods had accepted such important favors from the railroads that his impartiality was doubtful. Their irregular procedure in this case is therefore not surprising: Milchrist and Walker had prepared the application for the injunction, and the two judges had helped them to revise it before court opened. The breadth of their order was astonishing. Using the Sherman Antitrust Act of 1890 as authority, the injunction prohibited the strike leaders from any action to aid the boycott. They were forbidden to answer questions, to send telegrams. They were denied the right to urge men, by word of mouth, to join the boycott. Their constitutional rights to speak, write, and assemble freely, were ignored. They were, in short, completely shackled. Even Grover Cleveland was forced to admit that "a sweeping injunction had been granted against Eugene V. Debs. . . ."

FEDERAL INTERVENTION IN THE PULLMAN BOYCOTT

United States Strike Commission: THE INJUNCTION

United States Circuit Court,
District of Indiana

THE President of the United States of America to Eugene V. Debs, . . . , and the American Railway Union. And all other persons combining and conspiring with them, and to all other persons whomsoever:

You are hereby restrained, commanded, and enjoined absolutely to desist and refrain from in any way or manner interfering with, hindering, obstructing, or stopping any of the business of any of the following-named railroads: . . . [Twenty-three railroads are listed by name.] As common carriers of passengers and freight between or among any States of the United States, and from in any way interfering with, hindering, obstructing, or stopping any mail trains, express trains, whether freight or passenger, engaged in interstate commerce, or carrying passengers or freight between or among the States; and from in any manner interfering with, hindering, or stopping any trains carrying the mail, and from in any manner interfering with, hindering, obstructing, or stopping any engines, cars, or rolling stock of any of said companies engaged in interstate commerce, or in connection with the carriage of passengers or freight between or among the States; and from in any manner interfering with, injuring, or destroying any of the property of any of

said railroads engaged in or for the purposes of, or in connection with, interstate commerce, or the carriage of the mails of the United States or the transportation of passengers or freight between or among the States; and from entering upon the grounds or premises of any of said railroads for the purpose of interfering with, hindering, obstructing, or stopping any of said mail trains, passenger or freight trains engaged in interstate commerce, or in the transportation of passengers or freight between or among the States; or for the purpose of interfering with, injuring, or destroying any of said property so engaged in or used in connection with interstate commerce, or the transportation of passengers or property between or among the States; and from injuring or destroying any part of the tracks, roadbed or road, or permanent structures of said railroads; and from injuring, destroying, or in any way interfering with any of the signals or switches of any of said railroads; and from displacing or extinguishing any of the signals of any of said railroads, and from spiking, locking, or in any manner fastening any of the switches of any of said railroads, and from uncoupling or in any way hampering or obstructing the control by any of said railroads of any of the cars, engines, or parts of trains of any of said railroads engaged in interstate commerce or in the transportation of passengers or freight between or among

U. S. Strike Commission Report, Senate Executive Document No. 7, 53d Congress, 3d session, pp. 179–180.

the States, or engaged in carrying any of the mails of the United States; and from compelling or inducing, or attempting to compel or induce, by threats, intimidation, persuasion, force, or violence, any of the employees of any of said railroads to refuse or fail to perform any of their duties as employees of any of said railroads in connection with the interstate business or commerce of such railroads, or the carriage of the United States mail by such railroads, or the transportation of passengers or property between or among the States; and from compelling or inducing, or attempting to compel or induce, by threats, intimidation, force, or violence, any of the employees of said railroads who are employed by such railroads and engaged in its service in the conduct of interstate business, or in the operation of any of its trains carrying the mail of the United States, or doing interstate business, or the transportation of passengers and freight between and among the States, to leave the service of such railroads, and from preventing any persons whatever, by threats, intimidation, force, or violence from entering the service of any of said railroads and doing the work thereof, in the carrying of the mails of the United States or the transportation of passengers and freight between or among the States; and from doing any act whatever in furtherance of any conspiracy or combination to restrain either of said railroad companies in the free and unhindered control and handling of interstate commerce over the lines of said railroads, and of transportation of persons and freight between and among the States; and from ordering, directing, aiding, assisting, or abetting, in any manner whatever, any person or persons to commit any or either of the acts aforesaid.

And Eugene V. Debs and all other persons are hereby enjoined and restrained from sending out any letters, messages, or communications directing, inciting, encouraging, or instructing any persons whatsoever to interfere with the business or affairs, directly or indirectly, of any of the railway companies hereinabove named, or from persuading any of the employees of said railway companies while in the employment of their respective companies to fail or refuse to perform the duties of their employment.

And it is further ordered, that the aforesaid injunction and writ of injunction shall be in force and binding upon such of said defendants as are named in said bill from and after the service upon them severally of said writ by delivering to them severally a copy of said writ, or by reading the same to them, and the service upon them respectively of the writ of subpoena herein, and shall be binding upon said defendants whose names are alleged to be unknown, from and after the service of such writ upon them respectively, by the reading of the same to them, or by the publication thereof by posting or printing, and after service of subpoena on any of said defendants herein named shall be binding upon said defendants and upon all other persons whatsoever who are not named herein from and after the time when they shall severally have knowledge of the entry of such order and the existence of said injunction.

Witness Honorable Melville W. Fuller, Chief Justice of the Supreme Court of the United States, and the seal of the circuit court of the United States for the district of Indiana, this 3d day of July, A. D. 1894, and the one hundred and eighteenth year of the Independence of the United States of America.

Noble C. Butler, *Clerk.*

United States Supreme Court: IN RE DEBS

[ED.: On July 2, 1894, the district attorney for the Northern District of Illinois, under the direction of Attorney-General Richard Olney, filed a bill of complaint in the Circuit Court of the United States for the Northern District of Illinois against Debs and others for having entered into a combination and conspiracy to obstruct interstate commerce and requested an injunction. In response, the Court issued the injunction, the gist of which is reproduced in the foregoing pages.

Debs and other ARU officials were arrested and on December 14, 1894, were found guilty of contempt by the Circuit Court. They were sentenced to imprisonment in the county jail for terms varying from three to six months. On January 14, 1895, they applied to the Supreme Court for a writ of error — which was denied on January 17 — and also for a writ of habeas corpus. The case was argued March 25, 26, 1895, and the decision handed down May 27, 1895. Excerpts from Lyman Trumbull's argument for Debs and his associates and the opinion of the Supreme Court as delivered by Mr. Justice Brewer are given below.]

MR. LYMAN TRUMBULL for petitioners.

I. . . . It was not unlawful for the American Railway Union to call off the members of the organization, although it might incidentally affect the operation of the railroads. Refusing to work for a railroad company is no crime, and though such action may incidentally delay the mails or interfere with interstate commerce, it being a lawful act, and not done for that purpose, is no offence.

II. In the proceeding now before the court the main question is whether the bill states a case over which a court of equity has jurisdiction; if not, then the injunction was void and the prisoners are entitled to their discharge. . . .

If the prisoners were guilty of an offence against the United States by any acts which interfered with the transportation of the mails, the laws provide for their punishment; but equity has no jurisdiction to grant an injunction to stay proceedings in a criminal matter. . . .

III. . . . The act to protect trade and commerce against unlawful restraints and monopolies does not apply to the case stated in the bill. If it does, then it is unconstitutional. If a court of equity is authorized to restrain and prevent persons from the commission of crimes or misdemeanors prohibited by law, it must have the power to enforce its restraining order. In this case some of the parties are sentenced to imprisonment for six months, and for what? For doing some of the things forbidden by a criminal statute. If they have done none of the things forbidden, they have not violated the injunction, for it could only restrain them from doing what the law forbade. It follows that by indirection a court of equity under its assumed jurisdiction to issue injunctions and punish for contempts, is made to execute a criminal statute and deprive persons of their liberty without a jury trial. This a court of equity has no power to do, nor is it competent for Congress to confer such a power on a court of equity.

MR. JUSTICE BREWER, after stating the case, delivered the opinion of the court.

The case presented by the bill is this:

Excerpted from "In Re Debs, Petitioner," *United States Reports,* Volume 158: Cases Adjudged in the Supreme Court at October Term, 1894 (New York: Banks & Brothers, 1895), pp. 564–600.

The United States, finding that the interstate transportation of persons and property, as well as the carriage of the mails,
is forcibly obstructed, and that a combination and conspiracy exists to subject
the control of such transportation to the
will of the conspirators, applied to one of
their courts, sitting as a court of equity,
for an injunction to restrain such obstruction and prevent carrying into effect such
conspiracy. Two questions of importance
are presented: First. Are the relations of
the general government to interstate
commerce and the transportation of the
mails such as authorize a direct interference to prevent a forcible obstruction
thereof? Second: If authority exists, as
authority in governmental affairs implies
both power and duty, has a court of
equity jurisdiction to issue an injunction
in aid of the performance of such duty?

First. What are the relations of the
general government to interstate commerce and the transportation of the
mails? They are those of direct super-
vision, control, and management. While
under the dual system which prevails
with us, the powers of government are
distributed between the State and the
Nation, and while the latter is properly
styled a government of enumerated
powers, yet within the limits of such
enumeration it has all the attributes of
sovereignty, and, in the exercise of those
enumerated powers, acts directly upon
the citizen, and not through the inter-
mediate agency of the State. . . .

Among the powers expressly given to
the national government are the control
of interstate commerce and the creation
and management of a post office system
for the nation. Article I, Section 8, of the
Constitution provides that "the Congress
shall have power. . . . Third, to regulate
commerce with foreign nations and

among the several States, and with the
Indian tribes. . . . Seventh, to establish
post offices and post roads."

Congress has exercised the power
granted in respect to interstate commerce in a variety of legislative acts. . . .

Under the power vested in Congress
to establish post offices and post roads,
Congress has, by a mass of legislation,
established the great post office system of
the country, with all its detail of organization, its machinery for the transaction
of business, defining what shall be carried and what not, and the prices of
carriage, and also prescribing penalties
for all offences against it. . . .

As, under the Constitution, power over
interstate commerce and the transportation of the mails is vested in the national
government, and Congress by virtue of
such grant has assumed actual and direct
control, it follows that the national government may prevent any unlawful and
forcible interference therewith. But how
shall this be accomplished? Doubtless,
it is within the competency of Congress
to prescribe by legislation that any interference with these matters shall be offences against the United States, and
prosecuted and punished by indictment
in the proper courts. But is that the only
remedy? Have the vast interests of the
nation in interstate commerce, and in the
transportation of the mails, no other protection than lies in the possible punishment of those who interfere with it? To
ask the question is to answer it. By
article 3, section 2, clause 3, of the Federal Constitution it is provided: "The
trial of all crimes except in cases of
impeachment shall be by jury; and such
trial shall be held in the State where the
said crime shall have been committed."
If all the inhabitants of a State, or even
a great body of them, should combine to

obstruct interstate commerce or the transportation of the mails, prosecutions for such offences had in such a community would be doomed in advance to failure. And if the certainty of such failure was known, and the national government had no other way to enforce the freedom of interstate commerce and the transportation of the mails than by prosecution and punishment for interference therewith, the whole interests of the nation in these respects would be at the absolute mercy of a portion of the inhabitants of that single State.

But there is no such impotency in the national government. The entire strength of the nation may be used to enforce in any part of the land the full and free exercise of all national powers and the security of all rights entrusted by the Constitution to its care. The strong arm of the national government may be put forth to brush away all obstructions to the freedom of interstate commerce or the transportation of the mails. If the emergency arises, the army of the Nation, and all its militia, are at the service of the Nation to compel obedience to its laws.

But passing to the second question, is there no other alternative than the use of force on the part of the executive authorities whenever obstructions arise to the freedom of interstate commerce or the transportation of the mails? Is the army the only instrument by which rights of the public can be enforced and the peace of the nation preserved? Grant that any public nuisance may be forcibly abated either at the instance of the authorities, or by any individual suffering private damage therefrom, the existence of this right of forcible abatement is not inconsistent with nor does it destroy the right of appeal in an orderly way to the courts for a judicial determination, and an exercise of their powers by writ of injunction and otherwise to accomplish the same result. . . .

So in the case before us, the right to use force does not exclude the right of appeal to the courts for a judicial determination and for the exercise of all their powers of prevention. Indeed, it is more to the praise than to the blame of the government, that, instead of determining for itself questions of right and wrong on the part of these petitioners and their associates and enforcing that determination by the club of the policeman and the bayonet of the soldier, it submitted all those questions to the peaceful determination of judicial tribunals, and invoked their consideration and judgment as to the measure of its rights and powers and the correlative obligations of those against whom it made complaint. And it is equally to the credit of the latter that the judgment of those tribunals was by the great body of them respected, and the troubles which threatened so much disaster terminated.

Neither can it be doubted that the government has such an interest in the subject-matter as enables it to appear as party plaintiff in this suit. It is said that equity only interferes for the protection of property, and that the government has no property interest. A sufficient reply is that the United States have a property in the mails, the protection of which was one of the purposes of this bill. . . .

We do not care to place our decision upon this ground alone. Every government, entrusted, by the very terms of its being, with powers and duties to be exercised and discharged for the general welfare, has a right to apply to its own courts for any proper assistance in the exercise of the one and the discharge of the other, and it is no sufficient answer to its appeal to one of those courts that it has no pecuniary interest in the matter. The obligation which it is under to promote the interest of all, and to prevent the wrongdoing of one resulting in injury to the general welfare, is often of itself sufficient to give it a standing in court. . . .

It is obvious . . . that while it is not the province of the government to interfere in any mere matter of private controversy between individuals, or to use its great powers to enforce the rights of one against another, yet, whenever the wrongs complained of are such as affect the public at large, and are in respect of matters which by the Constitution are entrusted to the care of the Nation, and concerning which the Nation owes the duty to all the citizens of securing to them their common rights, then the mere fact that the government has no pecuniary interest in the controversy is not sufficient to exclude it from the courts, or prevent it from taking measures therein to fully discharge those constitutional duties.

The national government, given by the Constitution power to regulate interstate commerce, has by express statute assumed jurisdiction over such commerce when carried upon railroads. It is charged, therefore, with the duty of keeping those highways of interstate commerce free from obstruction, for it has always been recognized as one of the powers and duties of a government to remove obstructions from the highways under its control. . . .

It is said that seldom have the courts assumed jurisdiction to restrain by injunction in suits brought by the government, either state or national, obstructions to highways, either artificial or natural. This is undoubtedly true, but

the reason is that the necessity for such interference has only been occasional. Ordinarily, the local authorities have taken full control over the matter, and by indictment for misdemeanor, or in some kindred way, have secured the removal of the obstruction and the cessation of the nuisance.

That the bill filed in this case alleged special facts calling for the exercise of all the powers of the court is not open to question. The picture drawn in it of the vast interests involved, not merely of the city of Chicago and the State of Illinois, but of all the States, and the general confusion into which the interstate commerce of the country was thrown; the forcible interference with that commerce; the attempted exercise by individuals of powers belonging only to government, and the threatened continuance of such invasions of public right, presented a condition of affairs which called for the fullest exercise of all the powers of the courts. If ever there was a special exigency, one which demanded that the court should do all that courts can do, it was disclosed by this bill, and we need not turn to the public history of the day, which only reaffirms with clearest emphasis all its allegations. . . .

Again, it is objected that it is outside of the jurisdiction of a court of equity to enjoin the commission of crimes. This, as a general proposition, is unquestioned. A chancellor has no criminal jurisdiction. Something more than the threatened commission of an offence against the laws of the land is necessary to call into exercise the injunctive powers of the court. There must be some interferences, actual or threatened, with property or rights of a pecuniary nature, but when such interferences appear the jurisdiction of a court of equity arises, and is not destroyed by the fact that they are accompanied by or are themselves violations of the criminal law. . . .

The law is full of instances in which the same act may give rise to a civil action and a criminal prosecution. . . . In such cases the jurisdiction of the civil court is invoked, not to enforce the criminal law and punish the wrongdoer, but to compensate the injured party for the damages which he or his property has suffered, and it is no defence to the civil action that the same act by the defendant exposes him also to indictment and punishment in a court of criminal jurisdiction. So here, the acts of the defendants may or may not have been violations of the criminal law. If they were, that matter is for inquiry in other proceedings. The complaint made against them in this is of disobedience to an order of a civil court, made for the protection of property and the security of rights. If any criminal prosecution be brought against them for the criminal offences alleged in the bill of complaint, of derailing and wrecking engines and trains, assaulting and disabling employees of the railroad companies, it will be no defence to such prosecution that they disobeyed the orders of injunction served upon them and have been punished for such disobedience.

Nor is there in this any invasion of the constitutional right of trial by jury. We fully agree with counsel that "it matters not what form the attempt to deny constitutional right may take. It is vain and ineffectual, and must be so declared by the courts," and we reaffirm the declaration made for the court . . . that "it is the duty of courts to be watchful for the constitutional rights of the citizen, and against any stealthy encroachments thereon. . . ." But the power of a court to make

an order carries with it the equal power to punish for a disobedience of that order, and the inquiry as to the question of disobedience has been, from time immemorial, the special function of the court. And this is no technical rule. In order that a court may compel obedience to its orders it must have the right to inquire whether there has been any disobedience thereof. To submit the question of disobedience to another tribunal, be it a jury or another court, would operate to deprive the proceeding of half its efficiency. . . .

In brief, a court, enforcing obedience to its orders by proceedings for contempt, is not executing the criminal laws of the land, but only securing to suitors the rights which it has adjudged them entitled to.

Further, it is said by counsel in their brief:

"No case can be cited where such a bill in behalf of the sovereign has been entertained against riot and mob violence, though occurring on the highway. . . ."

It must be borne in mind that this bill was not simply to enjoin a mob and mob violence. It was not a bill to command a keeping of the peace; much less was its purport to restrain the defendants from abandoning whatever employment they were engaged in. The right of any laborer, of any number of laborers, to quit work was not challenged. The scope and purpose of the bill was only to restrain forcible obstructions of the highways along which interstate commerce travels and the mails are carried. And the facts set forth at length are only those facts which tended to show that the defendants were engaged in such obstructions. . . .

We have given to this case the most careful and anxious attention, for we realize that it touches closely questions of supreme importance to the people of this country. Summing up our conclusions, we hold that the government of the United States is one having jurisdiction over every foot of soil within its territory, and acting directly upon each citizen; that while it is a government of enumerated powers, it has within the limits of those powers all the attributes of sovereignty; that to it is committed power over interstate commerce and the transmission of the mail; that the powers thus conferred upon the national government are not dormant, but have been assumed and put into practical exercise by the legislation of Congress; that in the exercise of those powers it is competent for the nation to remove all obstructions upon highways, natural or artificial, to the passage of interstate commerce or the carrying of the mail; that while it may be competent for the government (through the executive branch and in the use of the entire executive power of the nation) to forcibly remove all such obstructions, it is equally within its competency to appeal to the civil courts for an inquiry and determination as to the existence and character of any alleged obstructions, and if such are found to exist, or threaten to occur, to invoke the powers of those courts to remove or restrain such obstructions; that the jurisdiction of courts to interfere in such matters by injunction is one recognized from ancient times and by indubitable authority; that such jurisdiction is not ousted by the fact that the obstructions are accompanied by or consist of acts in themselves violations of the criminal law; that the proceeding by injunction is of a civil character, and may be enforced by proceedings in contempt; that such proceedings are not in execution of the criminal laws of the land;

that the penalty for a violation of injunction is no substitute for and no defence to a prosecution for any criminal offences committed in the course of such violation; that the complaint filed in this case clearly showed an existing obstruction of artificial highways for the passage of interstate commerce and the transmission of the mail — an obstruction not only temporarily existing, but threatening to continue; that under such complaint the Circuit Court had power to issue its process of injunction; that it having been issued and served on these defendants, the Circuit Court had authority to inquire whether its orders had been disobeyed, and when it found that they had been, then to proceed under section 725, Revised Statutes, which grants power "to punish, by fine or imprisonment, . . . disobedience, . . . by any party . . . or other person, to any lawful writ, process, order, rule, decree or command," and enter the order of punishment complained of; and, finally, that the Circuit Court, having full jurisdiction in the premises, its finding of the fact of disobedience is not open to review on *habeas corpus* in this or any other court. . . .

We enter into no examination of the act of July 2, 1890 [the Sherman Anti-Trust Act], . . . upon which the Circuit Court relied mainly to sustain its jurisdiction. It must not be understood from this that we dissent from the conclusions of that court in reference to the scope of the act, but simply that we prefer to rest our judgment on the broader ground which has been discussed in this opinion, believing it of importance that the principles underlying it should be fully stated and affirmed.

The petition for a writ of *habeas corpus* is *Denied.*

John P. Altgeld: COMMENT ON THE SUPREME COURT DECISION

GOVERNOR, what have you to say on the decisions of the United States Supreme Court in the Debs case?

The remanding of Debs to jail is in itself a matter of small consequence compared with the principle established, which is of transcendent importance. This decision marks a turning point in our history, for it establishes a new form of government never before heard of among men, that is government by injunction. Under this procedure a federal judge sitting in a rear room can on motion of some corporation lawyer issue a ukase which he calls an injunction forbidding anything he chooses to and which the law does not forbid. Where the law forbids a thing no injunction is necessary. In other words he can legislate for himself, and having done so can then turn around and arrest and imprison as many people as he pleases; not for violating any law but on the mere pretext that they had disregarded his injunction, and, mark you, they are not tried by a jury according to the forms of law, but the same judge who issued the ukase and who claims that his dignity was offended himself tries the case, and whether anything is proven or nothing is proven he can send men to prison at pleasure and there is no remedy.

The provision of the Constitution "That no man shall be deprived of his liberty without a trial by an impartial jury" is practically wiped out by this decision of the United States Supreme Court and the theory that ours was exclusively a government of law is now at an end, for every community is now subject to obey any whim or caprice which any federal judge may promulgate. And if federal judges can do this then it will not be long until State judges will follow this example. The Constitution declares that our government has three departments, the legislative, judicial and executive, and that no one shall trench on the other, but under this new order of things a federal judge becomes at once a legislator, court and executioner.

For over a century our government moved along the lines of the Constitution and we became great and powerful. Life and property were protected and the law was enforced. Now we have made a departure, the bulwark of liberty has been undermined, trial by jury has been stricken down.

You know there were two separate proceedings against Debs. One was according to the established forms of law; he was indicted by a grand jury for acts alleged to have been committed during the strike, and he was regularly tried by a jury and it turned out there was absolutely no case against him. Nothing was proven. It is true the jury were not allowed to bring in a verdict because near the end of the trial one of the jurors became ill and the prosecution refused to go on. Debs' attorneys offered to proceed with the remaining eleven or to add a new man and proceed, but the railroad lawyer, who also represented the government, feeling that he had no case at all, would not consent, and he thereby prevented a verdict of acquittal and had the case postponed.

The other proceeding was by injunction. A federal judge on motion of some railroad attorneys issued a ukase against the people of all the States in that judicial circuit, in which he forbade nearly every-

John P. Altgeld, *Live Questions* (1899 ed.; Chicago: published by the author), pp. 450–461.

thing that the ingenuity of man could think of and which the law did not forbid, and having thus legislated he then turned around and had Debs and others arrested, not for violating any law but for failing to respect his ukase or injunction. And then this judge not only refused to give a jury trial but he himself proceeded to determine whether his own dignity had been offended, and he promptly sent the defendants to prison, the judge being legislator, court and executioner.

Had there been a jury trial the defendants would have been discharged, because it was not proved that they had violated any law. This would have been in harmony with the Constitution, with the law of the land with eternal justice. But the corporations wanted the Constitution brushed aside, and the federal judge kindly obliged them, and the Supreme Court has now approved his acts.

For a number of years it has been marked that the decisions of the United States courts were nearly always in favor of corporations. Then it was noticed that no man could be appointed to a federal judgeship unless he was satisfactory to those interests. Over a year ago the New York World talked about a packed Supreme Court, and that court has within a few days rendered two decisions which unfortunately tend to confirm this charge. A week ago it did violence to the Constitution and laws of the land by holding that the government had no power to tax the rich of this country. Now it has stricken down trial by jury and has established government by injunction.

Forty years ago the slave power predominated; to-day it is capitalism.

George William Curtis described the slave power of forty years ago as follows:

"Slavery sat in the White House and made laws in the capitol; courts of justice were its ministers and legislatures were its lackeys. It silenced the preacher in the pulpit; it muzzled the editor at his desk and the professor in his lecture-room. It set the price upon the heads of peaceful citizens; it robbed the mails and denounced the vital principles of the Declaration of Independence as treason. Even in States whose laws did not tolerate slavery it ruled the club and the drawing-room, the factory and the office. It swaggered at the dinner table and scourged with scorn a cowardly society. It tore the golden rule from school books and the pictured benignity of Christ from the prayer book."

Now substitute the word "capitalism" for the word "slavery" and the above is an exact picture of our condition to-day. The American people crushed the slave power, they washed its stain off our flag and saved our institutions. Can they rescue them again? Many say yes, but they have not reflected that the crushing force which now confronts them is greater than was ever the slave power. Besides, slavery itself was sectional and in the end it was possible to unite the rest of the country against it. But the corrupt money power has its withering finger on every pulse in the land and is destroying the rugged manhood and love of liberty which alone can carry a people through a great crisis. What, then, is the situation to-day? For over twenty years foreign and domestic capitalism has dominated. "It sits in the White House and legislates in the capitol. Courts of justice are its ministers and legislatures are its lackeys." And the whole machinery of fashionable society is its handmaid. . . .

John P. Altgeld: FEDERAL INTERFERENCE IN THE CHICAGO STRIKE

I AM aware that by persistent vilification and deliberate misrepresentation the partisan press has made the impression upon the minds of many good citizens that I, as Governor of Illinois, during the railroad disturbances of two years ago, did not do my duty and did not make the proper effort to protect life and property in Chicago, but sympathized with lawlessness and disorder; that federal interference was necessary to save the city. If there were even a semblance of truth in this, then no condemnation could be too severe, for a government that will not promptly and thoroughly protect life and property and preserve law and order is an abomination and should be wiped off of the earth. But, let us see what the indisputable facts are as shown by the records, and then you can judge for yourselves. . . .

In order to give you a more comprehensive view of the situation, I remind you that during the several months immediately prior to the beginning of the railroad strike there prevailed in all of the coal mining States a great coal miners' strike. . . . During that long strike order was maintained everywhere [in Illinois], railroad trains were moved, and in those instances where depredations had been committed stealthily all the offenders were arrested and immediately lodged in jail and were punished. . . .

No sooner was this coal strike over than the great railroad strike began, and the operatives or trainmen of nearly all the great railroads of the country stopped work. This left the railroads helpless. . . . The railroad operatives, partly out of respect for the law and partly because they felt that violence would injure their cause, were orderly, but in centers of population, where there were great numbers of idle men drawn together by the excitement, a vicious element sometimes became demonstrative, and after the roads succeeded in getting new men to man some of their trains there were efforts made by the mob to prevent the moving of Pullman cars, and this in some cases precipitated trouble. Under the laws of Illinois, whenever the civil authorities are not able to maintain order or enforce the law, the Governor can order out troops for their assistance on the application of either the sheriff of the county, the mayor of a city or village, the county judge or the coroner. The constitution and laws of that State, in harmony with the Constitution and laws of the federal government, are based upon the principle that in a republic in time of peace the military should be subject to the civil officers and that the maintenance of law and order should in the first instance devolve upon the local officers in each community.

Early in this railroad strike and before there had been any serious disturbances in Chicago, applications for assistance were made by the local civil officers of five or six different railroad centers throughout the State and troops were promptly sent to their assistance, always arriving on the ground within a few hours after they had been applied for. . . .

In several instances troops had been asked for to protect railroad property and were promptly furnished, and it was then

Excerpts from a speech at Cooper Union, N. Y., October 17, 1896, reproduced in John P. Altgeld, *Live Questions* (1899 ed.; Chicago: published by the author), pp. 650–679.

found that the railroad companies had no men who were willing to work, and we had to find soldiers who had to act as brakemen and engineers in order to transport the troops. Several weeks prior to these dates, while the coal strike was pending, the Hon. William J. Allen, United States District Judge at Springfield, Ill., finding that the marshal was having trouble to carry out some of the orders of his court, wrote to the Attorney General at Washington upon the subject of receiving assistance from federal troops to enforce the orders of the United States court, and the Attorney General sent the following dispatch:

Washington, D. C., June 16, 1894.
Allen, United States Judge,
Springfield, Illinois:
I understand the State of Illinois is willing to protect property against lawless violence with military force if necessary. Please advise receivers to take proper steps to procure protection by civil authorities of the State. If such protection proves inadequate, the government should be applied to for military assistance.
OLNEY, Attorney General.

This laid down the correct doctrine, that is, that the local authorities should be applied to first, and in case of their failure, then the Governor of the State should be applied to for assistance. Immediately after the date of this telegram, and on several occasions thereafter during the coal strike, as well as on several occasions during the subsequent railroad strike, prior to the serious disturbances in Chicago, the United States Marshal for the Southern District of Illinois applied to the Governor for military aid to enable him and his deputies to execute the processes of the United States court, and in each instance troops were promptly sent to his assistance. This, in brief,

shows the attitude of the State administration toward that part of the State lying outside of Chicago, and as troops were always promptly furnished where needed, and in every instance were promptly furnished to the United States Marshal when asked for to assist him in enforcing the orders of the United States court for Southern Illinois, and as the State administration stood equally ready to furnish any assistance which the United States Marshal at Chicago might require to carry out the orders of the United States court there, and inasmuch as Attorney General Olney had only a few weeks before telegraphed that the Governor should be applied to for troops to assist in carrying out the orders of the United States court, it would naturally be expected that if the United States Marshal at Chicago should need assistance that he would apply for such assistance to the Governor of the State. But instead of pursuing this course, just the opposite course was pursued. No application of any sort for troops was made to the Governor by the United States Marshal or any of the United States authorities at Chicago, nor was any such application made by any of the local city or county officers of Chicago until the 6th of July, and then such application was made on my suggestion.

You may ask why the federal administration at Washington did not direct the United States Marshal at Chicago to apply to the State for troops in order to enforce the orders of the United States courts there, just as the United States Marshal for Southern Illinois had applied to the State for troops to enforce the orders of the United States courts at that place. I will tell you. It subsequently developed that more than ten days before there was any trouble the corporations of Chicago applied to the federal government for troops so that a precedent might be set under which they could in the future appeal directly in all cases to the federal government and become independent of local governments.

Thereupon, more than five days in advance of any trouble in Chicago, Mr. Olney and Mr. Cleveland decided to reverse the policy and practice of the government and take an entire new departure by setting a precedent of having the President to interfere at pleasure and having the United States courts and the United States government take the corporations directly under their wings in the first instance in all cases, and in order to have the American people submit to the violation of the Constitution and laws of the land as well as of every principle of self-government, the trouble at Chicago was, by systematic effort and deliberate misrepresentation, so magnified as to make it seem that we were bordering on anarchy, and that consequently federal interference was necessary. The impression was sought to be made upon the country that we were bordering on civil war and the destruction of society and that neither the local authorities nor the State authorities were willing to maintain law and order, while the real fact was that the federal government took steps to interfere in Chicago before there was any rioting or any serious trouble of any kind, and that the State authorities, who stood ready to act promptly, were intentionally ignored. . . .

The government already had a United States District Attorney with a large number of assistants in that city [Chicago] who were amply able to attend to all of the government business there, but instead of simply increasing their number, Attorney General Olney and President Cleveland decided to appoint a special counsel who should still more

directly represent the government during this strike. The administration claimed to be Democratic. There were hundreds of able and distinguished Democratic lawyers in Chicago whose appointment would have carried confidence, but the administration would not have any of these. The Attorney General and the President evidently felt that when the Constitution and the laws were to be trampled on, when the precedents and traditions of the government were to be disregarded and a new and a revolutionary policy was to be inaugurated, that they needed a Republican for that purpose. Here again there were hundreds of able and distinguished Republican lawyers in Chicago who were not connected with corporations, who were in no way involved in the strike on either side and whose appointment would at least have aroused no suspicion; but the Attorney General and the President evidently felt that they would not do, that for the particular work which they wanted done they needed a corporation lawyer, and here again there were a large number of able and distinguished corporation lawyers in Chicago who were Republicans and who were in no way involved in the strike on either side; but the Attorney General and the President evidently felt that for the peculiar and revolutionary work they wanted done these men might not be reliable. So they rejected these and appointed Mr. Walker, who was not only a Republican and a corporation lawyer, but who was at that time the attorney for a great railroad that was directly involved in the strike, so that he himself was already involved in the controversy, he on one side and the railroad employes on the other. In other words the Attorney General and the President took one of the parties to the controversy and placed at its disposal

United States Marshals, United States courts and the United States army. Never before in the history of our country were the courts, the grand juries, the United States Marshals and the United States army stripped of all semblance of impartiality and given as a convenience to one of the parties.

This, bear in mind, was on the first day of July, three days ahead of any rioting and five days in advance of any serious rioting, and on the same day the United States troops at Fort Sheridan, within an hour's run of Chicago, were ordered to be in readiness to go to that city on a moment's notice. The plan determined upon was to have United States courts issue blanket injunctions . . . against the strikers and all other people, forbidding everything imaginable, and then use the marshals for the purpose of carrying out these injunctions and use the federal troops for this and other purposes. Up to this time neither the Republican sheriff of the county nor Mr. Hopkins, the Democratic mayor of the city, nor any other local State official, nor any federal official at Chicago or elsewhere had applied to the Governor for troops. . . .

Immediately after the beginning of the strike in which the railway operatives refused to work, the managers of the railway lines entering Chicago formed an organization to fight the strike, and they met towards the close of each day to report upon the situation, and at 6 o'clock p.m. of July 2, the day after the special counsel had been appointed by the government, and the day after the troops at Fort Sheridan had been ordered to be in readiness at Chicago, they met and reported as to the condition of their roads and the following copies of reports made by themselves, which are samples of all the reports, show the situation at that time:

Wisconsin Central: "All passenger and freight trains moving and business resumed its normal condition."

Chicago & Northern Pacific: "Suburban trains all running about on time. Freight moving without interruption. Night suburban trains discontinued for fear of being stoned by loafers."

[ED. Altgeld cites similar reports from six other roads.]

This was on the evening of July 2d, and corroborates the statement made by the fire department that for the first three days in July no attempt was made to destroy railroad property. In those cases where a road was not attempting to move freight it was due to the fact that their old hands had quit work and they had not yet been able to get new ones.

On the morning of July 3d, being the morning after the railroad managers had reported the conditions of their roads, as already shown, and before anything further had developed, Mr. Walker, the special counsel, dictated a dispatch which was sent to Washington, asking that federal troops be sent into the city, and on the afternoon of the 3d, the federal troops appeared in Chicago and camped on the Lake Front and ostensibly went on duty. Let me repeat here that up to this time there had been no serious disturbance of mails, no destruction of property and according to the reports of the railroad managers themselves no serious interference with the operation of the railroads or with interstate commerce.

And let me also repeat that up to this time the State and local authorities had been completely ignored, the State was not asked to do anything or to assist in any manner, although it was not only able to entirely control the situation, but stood ready to do it. . . .

At about 6 o'clock on the evening of July 3d, about the time the United States troops were entering Chicago, the managers of the different railroads again met and reported in substance as follows:

Santa Fe: "Six regular passenger trains on time; moving freight."

Chicago, Milwaukee & St. Paul: "All passengers on time and without interference; moving freight."

Chicago & Alton: "Trains stop for want of firemen."

Baltimore & Ohio: "Trains moving; one engine detached by withdrawal of coupling pin; police detailed and protected train at once. . . ."

[Altgeld gives similar reports for twelve additional roads, three of which cite trouble elsewhere but not at Chicago.]

On the 4th of July there was some disturbance, although the federal troops were on the ground, but instead of overawing the mob they seemed to act only as an irritant to intensify the situation, and on the evening of the 4th of July the managers again met and reported in substance as follows: . . .

[Of the thirteen reports which Altgeld quotes, that of the Chicago, Burlington & Quincy is perhaps typical:]

. . . "Had trouble in attempting to move a freight train; last night Pullman cars were cut from passenger train, but with assistance of police were promptly recoupled and train moved forward; all other trains of last night and to-day are running without interference of any kind. The entire force of switchmen in St. Louis left the service of the road yesterday evening. We are not trying to handle freight to-day; everything is quiet."

On the 5th of July the conditions were about the same as on the 4th, but there were rumors of an extension of the strike, and it is evident that the federal troops were doing no good there. On the morning of the 6th of July the President of the Illinois Central Railroad telegraphed me

that the property of his road was being destroyed by a mob and that he could not get protection. I wired him at once to get some one of the local authorities who are authorized to ask for troops to do so, and that if all should refuse, to wire me that fact, and that we would furnish protection promptly. I took the position as a matter of law that if the local authorities failed to protect property and enforce the law and refused to apply for State aid while property is actually being destroyed and the peace is being disturbed, that then the Governor of the State not only has the right, but it is his duty to see that order is restored and the law enforced, and therefore I sent that telegram. At the same time I sent a telegram to a friend in Chicago requesting him to at once see Mayor Hopkins and tell him that it seemed to me the situation was serious and that he had better apply to the State for aid. This message was at once communicated to Mayor Hopkins, and about noon on that day, being the 6th of July, the day on which the property was destroyed, the mayor telegraphed for troops and by sundown on that day we had put over 5,000 State troops on duty in Chicago, although some of them had to be transported 150 miles to reach the city. Never were troops moved with greater celerity. They at once got the situation under control and stopped the rioting, but they found that one of the railroad yards in which a fire had broken out was far out on the prairie and had an insufficient supply of water; that the fire department was unable to put out the fire and thus prevent the destruction of some cars that took fire from others that were burning. Within twenty-four hours after the State troops arrived on the ground the rioting was suppressed. There were still a few cases, during the following days, of stealthy incendiarism, but no more forcible resistance. . . .

Up to this time the United States Marshal at Chicago, instead of calling on the State for assistance, as the marshal for Southern Illinois had done, had sworn in an army of over 4,000 deputy marshals to assist him in carrying out the injunctions which had been issued by the courts. . . . not withstanding their number they did not seem to accomplish anything. The disturbances kept growing and spreading. . . . it devolved in the end upon the police and State troops, the properly and regularly constituted authorities, to restore order.

Speaking of the work of the federal troops in Chicago, it will be seen by the record that they did no good. They were ordered to be in readiness five days in advance of any trouble, and were actually on the ground on the 3d day of July, before there had been any serious disturbance of any kind, and they remained on the ground for weeks thereafter. Yet instead of overawing the mob or exerting an influence for good, their presence added to the excitement and served as an irritant, and instead of suppressing rioting it will be noticed that it did not begin until after their arrival and then grew steadily, and on the 6th, the worst day, instead of suppressing they accomplished nothing. The federal soldiers and their officers were no doubt brave men and good soldiers, but they, like the deputy marshals, were occupying an anomalous position, and were therefore under a disadvantage. . . . So far as can be learned, their presence did not prevent the burning of a single freight car in Chicago, they accomplished nothing, yet during all this time the impression was made on the country that President Cleveland and the federal troops were saving Chicago. General Miles was in

command, and his headquarters seemed to be, for a number of days, a regular newspaper bureau, and there was an apparent effort on the part of some people to make an impression throughout the East that civil war was raging in Chicago, and the General and President Cleveland vied with each other in claiming the credit of suppressing that war. . . . The fact is that up to the time the State troops appeared upon the scene the police force of Chicago alone did all of any value that was done to maintain law and order.

The only officer who attempted to make any report of the things actually done by the federal troops in Chicago was Captain J. M. Lee, assistant to Inspector General. . . . Captain Lee says that from July 4th to 20th he was constantly with the troops in Chicago. That duties consisted in communicating verbal orders and instructions of the commanding general to officers in command; also in accompanying troops to the riotous districts, selecting camps and stations and "in investigating and reporting upon the grave situations from day to day." It is clear that he would know of all that the troops did do. And as the whole report shows an effort to magnify every incident and make the most possible out of the occasion, we may feel certain that he told all he knew.

. . . Yet, so far as appears from his report, the federal troops did not prevent the burning of one car or the ditching of a single engine. If they were there to protect property or commerce why did they not at least make an effort on that day [July 6th, the day the destruction was heaviest]? . . .

General Miles, in the report already referred to, does not mention anything in particular that the federal troops did. But after speaking of their discipline says: "And their actions have very greatly contributed to the maintenance of civil law and in my opinion saved this country from a serious rebellion when one had been publicly declared to exist by one most responsible for its existence." This is extraordinary language and in view of the fact that there was no disturbance whatever of any kind in the city proper, that the rioting was at the stock yards and in the railroad yards on the prairies on the outskirts of the city; in view of the comparatively small damage done as found by the federal commission appointed by President Cleveland to investigate the whole matter, and as also found by the Chicago fire department, and in view of the written statements of Louis L. Troy, the superintendent of mails, that there had at no time been any considerable delay in moving the mails; and in view of the written reports of the railroad managers themselves that there was comparatively little interruption of their business, and finally, in view of the report made by Captain Lee at the time this language of General Miles seems absurd and must tend to destroy confidence in his judgment or else create the conviction that he was trying to make a false impression for the sake of getting a little glory thereby.

It is a matter of gratification to every patriotic citizen of Illinois that it was the State troops and the local civil authorities that restored law and order in that city. While they were not petted by fashionable society and were given very stinted praise by the newspapers, they did deal directly with the mob and restored order. During the trouble thousands of men all over the State tendered their services to the Governor, and I am satisfied that an army of two hundred thousand men could have been mustered in a few days if they had been called for. . . .

On the 5th day of July, 1894, after the federal troops had gone on duty in Chicago, I sent the following protest to the President and asked him to remove the troops:

Executive Office, State of Illinois,
July 5, 1894.
Hon. Grover Cleveland,
President of the United States,
Washington, D. C.
Sir: I am advised that you have ordered Federal troops to go into service in the State of Illinois. Surely the facts have not been correctly presented to you in this case, or you would not have taken this step, for it is entirely unnecessary, and, as it seems to me, unjustifiable. Waiving all questions of courtesy, I will say that the State of Illinois is not only able to take care of itself, but it stands ready to furnish the Federal Government any assistance it may need elsewhere. Our military force is ample, and consists of as good soldiers as can be found in the country. They have been ordered promptly whenever and wherever they were needed. . . . They have been ready every moment to go on duty, and have been and are now eager to go into service, but they have not been ordered out because nobody in Cook county, whether official or private citizen, asked to have their assistance, or even intimated in any way that their assistance was desired or necessary.

So far as I have been advised, the local officials have been able to handle the situation. But if any assistance were needed, the State stood ready to furnish 100 men for every one man required, and stood ready to do so at a moment's notice. Notwithstanding these facts the Federal Government has been applied to by men who had political and selfish motives for wanting to ignore the State government. . . . We have now had ten days of the railroad strike, and we have promptly furnished military aid wherever the local officials needed it.

In two instances the United States Marshal for the Southern District of Illinois applied for assistance to enable him to enforce the processes of the United States court, and troops were promptly furnished him, and he was assisted in every way he desired. The law has been thoroughly executed, and every man guilty of violating it during the strike has been brought to justice. If the marshal of the Northern District of Illinois or the authorities of Cook county needed military assistance they had but to ask for it in order to get it from the State.

At present some of our railroads are paralyzed, not by reason of obstruction, but because they cannot get men to operate their trains. For some reason they are anxious to keep this fact from the public and for this purpose they are making an outcry about obstructions in order to divert attention. Now, I will cite to you two examples which illustrate the situation:

Some days ago I was advised that the business of one of our railroads was obstructed at two railroad centers, and that there was a condition bordering on anarchy there, and I was asked to furnish protection so as to enable the employés of the road to operate the trains. Troops were promptly ordered to both points. Then it transpired that the company had not sufficient men on its line to operate one train. All the old hands were orderly, but refused to go to work. The company had large shops which worked a number of men who did not belong to the Railway Union and who could run an engine. They were appealed to to run the train but flatly refused. We were obliged to hunt up soldiers who could run an engine and operate a train. Again, two days ago, appeals which were almost frantic came from the officials of another road stating that at an important point on their line, trains were forcibly obstructed, and that there was a reign of anarchy at that place, and they asked for protection so that they could move their trains. Troops were put on the ground in a few hours' time, when the officer in command telegraphed me that there was no trouble, and had been none at that point, but that the road seemed to have no men to run trains, and the sheriff telegraphed that he did not need troops, but would himself move every train if the company would only furnish an engineer. The result was that the troops were there twelve hours before a single train was moved, although there was no attempt at interference by anybody.

It is true that in several instances a road made efforts to work a few green men and a crowd standing around insulted them and tried to drive them away, and in a few other cases they cut off Pullman sleepers from trains. But all these troubles were local in character and could easily be handled by the State authorities. Illinois has more railroad men than any other State in the Union, but as a rule they are orderly and well-behaved. This is shown by the fact that so very little actual violence has been committed. Only a very small percentage of these men have been guilty of infractions of the law. The newspaper accounts have in many cases been pure fabrications, and in others wild exaggerations.

I have gone thus into details to show that it is not soldiers that the railroads need so much as it is men to operate the trains, and that the conditions do not exist here which bring the cause within the Federal statute, a statute that was passed in 1881 and was in reality a war measure. The statute authorized the use of Federal troops in a State whenever it shall be impracticable to enforce the laws of the United States within such States by the ordinary judicial proceedings. Such a condition does not exist in Illinois. There have been a few local disturbances, but nothing that seriously interfered with the administration of justice, or that could not be easily controlled by the local or State authorities, for the Federal troops can do nothing that the State troops cannot do.

I repeat that you have been imposed upon in this matter, but even if by a forced construction it were held that the conditions here came within the letter of the statute, then I submit that local self-government is a fundamental principle of our Constitution. Each community shall govern itself so long as it can and is ready and able to enforce the law, and it is in harmony with this fundamental principle that the statute authorizing the President to send troops into States must be construed; especially is this so in matters relating to the exercise of the police power and the preservation of law and order.

To absolutely ignore a local government in matters of this kind, when the local government is ready to furnish assistance needed, and is amply able to enforce the law, not only insults the people of this State by imputing to them an inability to govern themselves, or an unwillingness to enforce the law, but is in violation of a basic principle of our institutions. The question of Federal supremacy is in no way involved. No one disputes it for a moment, but, under our Constitution, Federal supremacy and local self-government must go hand in hand, and to ignore the latter is to do violence to the Constitution.

As Governor of the State of Illinois, I protest against this, and ask the immediate withdrawal of the Federal troops from active duty in this State. Should the situation at any time get so serious that we cannot control it with the State forces, we will promptly ask for Federal assistance, but until such time, I protest, with all due deference, against this uncalled for reflection upon our people, and again ask the immediate withdrawal of these troops. I have the honor to be, yours respectfully,

JOHN P. ALTGELD, Governor of Illinois

Executive Mansion, Washington,
July 5, 1894

Hon. John P. Altgeld,
Governor of Illinois,
Springfield, Ill.:

Sir: Federal Troops were sent to Chicago in strict accordance with the Constitution and laws of the United States, upon the demand of the postoffice department that obstruction of the mails should be removed, and upon the representations of the judicial officers of the United States that the process of the Federal courts could not be executed through the ordinary means, and upon competent proof that conspiracies existed against commerce between the States. To meet these conditions, which are clearly within the province of Federal authority, the presence of Federal troops in the city of Chicago was

deemed not only proper, but necessary, and there has been no intention of thereby interfering with the plain duty of the local authorities to preserve the peace of the city.

GROVER CLEVELAND

To the Hon. Grover Cleveland,
President of the United States,
Washington, D. C.:

Sir: Your answer to my protest involves some startling conclusions and ignores and evades the question at issue — that is that the principle of local self-government is just as fundamental in our institutions as is that of Federal supremacy.

First — You calmly assume that the executive has the legal right to order Federal troops into any community of the United States, in the first instance, whenever there is the slightest disturbance, and that he can do this without any regard to the question as to whether that community is able to and ready to enforce the law itself, and, inasmuch as the executive is the sole judge of the question as to whether any disturbance exists or not in any part of the country, this assumption means that the executive can send Federal troops into any community in the United States at his pleasure, and keep them there as long as he chooses. If this is the law, then the principle of self-government either never did exist in this country or else has been destroyed, for no community can be said to possess local self-government, if the executive can, at his pleasure, send military forces to patrol its streets under pretense of enforcing some law. The kind of local self-government that could exist under these circumstances can be found in any of the monarchies of Europe, and it is not in harmony with the spirit of our institutions.

Second — It is also a fundamental principle in our government that except in times of war the military shall be subordinate to the civil authority. In harmony with this provision, the State troops are ordered out to act under and with the civil authorities. The troops you have ordered to Chicago are not under the civil authorities, and are in no way responsible to them for their conduct. They are not even acting under the United States Marshal or any Federal officer of the State, but are acting directly under military orders issued from military headquarters at Washington, and in so far as these troops act at all, it is military government.

Third — The Statute authorizing Federal troops to be sent into States in certain cases contemplates that the State troops shall be taken first. This provision has been ignored and it is assumed that the executive is not bound by it. Federal interference with industrial disturbances in the various States is certainly a new departure, and it opens up so large a field that it will require a very little stretch of authority to absorb to itself all the details of local government.

Fourth — You say that troops were ordered into Illinois upon the demand of the post-office department, and upon representations of the judicial officers of the United States that process of the courts could not be served, and upon proof that conspiracies existed. We will not discuss the facts, but look for a moment at the principle involved in your statement. All of these officers are appointed by the executive. Most of them can be removed by him at will. They are not only obliged to do his bidding, but they are in fact a part of the executive. If several of them can apply for troops, one alone can; so that under the law, as you assume it to be, an executive, through any one of his appointees, can apply to himself to have the military sent into any city or number of cities, and base his application on such representations as he sees fit to make. In fact, it will be immaterial whether he makes any showing or not, for the executive is the sole judge, and nobody else has any right to interfere or even inquire about it. Then the executive can pass on his own application — his will being the sole guide — he can hold the application to be sufficient, and order troops to as many places as he wishes and put them in command of any one he chooses, and have them act, not under the civil officers, either Federal or State, but directly under military orders from Washington, and there is not in the Constitution or laws, whether written or unwritten,

any limitation or restraint upon his power. His judgment, that is, his will, is the sole guide, and it being purely a matter of discretion, his decision can never be examined or questioned.

This assumption as to the power of the executive is certainly new, and I respectfully submit that it is not the law of the land. The jurists have told us that this is a government of law, and not a government by the caprice of an individual, and, further, instead of being autocratic, it is a government of limited power. Yet the autocrat of Russia could certainly not possess, or claim to possess, greater power than is possessed by the executive of the United States, if your assumption is correct.

Fifth — The executive has the command not only of the regular forces of all the United States, but of the military forces of all the States, and can order them to any place he sees fit; and as there are always more or less local disturbances over the country, it will be an easy matter under your construction of the law for an ambitious executive to order out the military forces of all of the States, and establish at once a military government. The only chance of failure in such a movement could come from rebellion, and with such a vast military power at command this could readily be crushed, for, as a rule, soldiers will obey orders.

As for the situation in Illinois, that is of no consequence now compared with the far-reaching principle involved. True, according to my advices, Federal troops have now been on duty for over two days, and although the men were brave and the officers valiant and able, yet their very presence proved to be an irritant because it aroused the indignation of a large class of people, who, while upholding law and order, had been taught to believe in local self-government and, therefore, resented what they regarded as unwarranted interference.

Inasmuch as the Federal troops can do nothing but what the State troops can do there, and believing that the State is amply able to take care of the situation and to enforce the law, and believing that the ordering out of the Federal troops was unwarranted, I again ask their withdrawal.

    (Signed)   JOHN P. ALTGELD

When all of the facts pertaining to the situation in Chicago are brought out it becomes apparent that if you were to concede the right of the President to send troops to any part of the Union whenever he pleased and on any pretext he pleased, there was no occasion for sending them to Chicago at all and especially not at the time that the order was given, which was in advance of any trouble. . . .

The act of the President was an entirely new departure in the history of our government. . . . Nobody for a moment questions the supremacy of the Union. But it does involve the question whether, in connection with federal supremacy, there does not go hand in hand the principle of local self-government. . . . Without federal union there must follow anarchy, and without local self-government there must follow despotism. . . . Local self-government is the very foundation of freedom and of republican institutions, and no people possess this who are subject to have the army patrol their streets, acting not under, but independently of the local authorities, and do this at the mere discretion of one man, or of a central power that is far away. . . .

The laws of Congress are the laws of each State and of each city just as much as the acts of the State legislature or of a city council. And it is the duty of a State and of a city to execute and enforce the laws of Congress just as much as it is to enforce the local laws. In this respect there is no distinction between laws. The mere fact that the federal government as a matter of expediency has seen fit to create judicial machinery to enforce the laws of the United States does not relieve a State nor even a city

of the fundamental duty of enforcing the laws of the United States. . . .

Local self government means that a municipality or a State shall use all the power in its possession to enforce all laws that are in force within its borders whether they be federal, State or municipal, and if the power of the State is inadequate for this purpose then the Constitution has provided a method for bringing in federal troops.

It is as much the duty of the State to furnish all necessary force to execute the process of a federal court held within its borders as it is to furnish the necessary force to execute the process of a State tribunal. Mr. Olney clearly recognized this principle when he telegraphed Judge Allen of the United States court at Springfield that the United States marshal of that district should apply to the State for the necessary assistance to execute the process and the decrees of the United States courts. . . .

It has been asked: "Suppose the officials and the people of a State in time of trouble refuse to enforce the law and refuse to ask for federal assistance, then must you let all society go to destruction?" You might as well ask, "Suppose the President failed or refused to do his duty then would the republic perish and all society be destroyed?"

This idea is absurd and grows out of the assumption that we exist and are held together by a force coming from above, instead of governing ourselves. It assumes that seventy millions of people may go to destruction and free institutions be destroyed unless some official reaches out and saves them. It ignores the fact that our government is founded on the theory that the people themselves do the governing and that the world's experience has shown that they can be trusted a thousand times over rather than some office-holder, and it further ignores the fact that for one hundred and twenty years the people of this country have so governed themselves, and that it was during this time that our institutions were developed, our cities were built and our greatness was achieved.

Grover Cleveland: THE GOVERNMENT IN THE CHICAGO STRIKE OF 1894

IN the last days of June, 1894, a very determined and ugly labor disturbance broke out in the city of Chicago. Almost in a night it grew to full proportions of malevolence and danger. Rioting and violence were its early accompaniments; and it spread so swiftly that within a few days it had reached nearly the entire Western and Southwestern sections of our country. Railroad transportation was especially involved in its attacks. The carriage of United States mails was interrupted, interstate commerce was obstructed, and railroad property was riotously destroyed.

This disturbance is often called "The Chicago Strike." It is true that its beginning was in that city; and the headquarters of those who inaugurated it and directed its operations were located there; but the name thus given to it is an entire misnomer so far as it applies to the scope and reach of the trouble. Railroad operations were more or less affected in twenty-seven States and Territories; and in all these the interposition of the general Government was to a greater or less extent invoked.

This wide-spread trouble had its inception in a strike by the employees of the Pullman Palace Car Company, a corporation located and doing business at the town of Pullman, which is within the limits of the city of Chicago. This company was a manufacturing corporation — or at least it was not a railroad corporation. . . .

The strike on the part of the employees of this company began on the eleventh day of May, 1894, and was provoked by a reduction of wages.

The American Railway Union was organized in the summer of 1893. It was professedly an association of all the different classes of railway employees. In its scope and intent it was the most compact and effective organization of the kind ever attempted. Its purpose was a thorough unification of defensive and offensive effort among railway employees under one central direction, and the creation of a combination embracing all such employees, which should make the grievances of any section of its membership a common cause. Those prominent in this project estimated that various other organizations of railroad employees then existing had a membership of 102,000 in the United States and neighboring countries; and they claimed that these brotherhoods, because of divided councils and for other reasons, were ineffective, and that nearly 1,000,000 railroad employees still remained unorganized.

The wonderful growth of this new combination is made apparent by the fact that between the month of August, 1893, and the time it became involved in the Pullman strike, in June, 1894, it had enrolled nearly 150,000 members.

From Grover Cleveland, *Presidential Problems* (New York: The Century Co., copyright 1904), pp. 80–117. Reprinted by permission of the publishers, Appleton-Century-Crofts, Inc.

The employees of the Pullman Palace Car Company could not on any reasonable and consistent theory be regarded as eligible to membership in an organization devoted to the interests of railway employees; and yet, during the months of March, April, and May, 1894, it appears that nearly 4000 of these employees were enrolled in the American Railway Union.

This, to say the least of it, was an exceedingly unfortunate proceeding, since it created a situation which implicated in a comparatively insignificant quarrel between the managers of an industrial establishment and their workmen the large army of the Railway Union. It was the membership of these workmen in the Railway Union, and the union's consequent assumption of their quarrel, that gave it the proportions of a tremendous disturbance, paralyzing the most important business interests, obstructing the functions of the Government, and disturbing social peace and order.

No injury to the property of the Pullman Palace Car Company was done or attempted while the strike was confined to its employees; and during that time very little disorder of any kind occurred.

It so happened, however, that in June, 1894, after the strike at Pullman had continued for about one month, a regular stated convention of the American Railway Union was held in the city of Chicago, which was attended by delegates from local branches of the organization in different States, as well as by representatives of its members among the employees of the Pullman Palace Car Company. At this convention the trouble at Pullman was considered, and after earnest efforts on the part of the Railway Union to bring about a settlement, a resolution was, on the twenty-second day of June, passed by the convention, declaring that unless the Pullman Palace Car Company should adjust the grievances of its employees before noon of the twenty-sixth day of June, the members of the American Railway Union would, after that date, refuse to handle Pullman cars and equipment.

The twenty-sixth day of June arrived without any change in the attitude of the parties to the Pullman controversy; and thereupon the order made by the American Railway Union forbidding the handling of Pullman cars, became operative throughout its entire membership.

At this time the Pullman Palace Car Company was furnishing drawing-room and sleeping-car accommodations to the traveling public under contracts with numerous railway companies, and was covering by this service about one hundred and twenty-five thousand miles of railway, or approximately three-fourths of all the railroad mileage of the country. The same railroad companies which had contracted to use these Pullman cars upon their lines had contracts with the United States Government for the carriage of mails, and were, of course, also largely engaged in interstate commerce. It need hardly be said that, of necessity, the trains on which the mails were carried and which served the purpose of interstate commerce were, very generally, those to which the Pullman cars were also attached.

The President of the Railway Union was one Eugene V. Debs. In a sworn statement afterward made he gave the following description of the results of the interference of the union in the Pullman dispute:

The employees, obedient to the order of the convention, at once, on the 26th, refused to haul Pullman cars. The switchmen, in the first place, refused to attach a Pullman car to a train, and that is where the trouble began; and then, when a switchman would be discharged for that, they would all simultaneously quit, as they had agreed to do. One department after another was involved until the Illinois Central was practically paralyzed, and the Rock Island and other roads in their turn. Up to the first day of July, or after the strike had been in progress five days, the railway managers, as we believe, were completely defeated. Their immediate resources were exhausted, their properties were paralyzed, and they were unable to operate their trains. Our men were intact at every point, firm, quiet, and yet determined, and no sign of violence or disorder anywhere. That was the condition on the thirtieth day of June and the first day of July.

The officers of the Railway Union from their headquarters in the city of Chicago gave directions for the maintenance and management of the strike, which were quickly transmitted to distant railroad points and were there promptly executed. As early as the 28th of June, two days after the beginning of the strike ordered by the Railway Union at Chicago, information was received at Washington from the Post-Office Department that on the Southern Pacific System, between Portland and San Francisco, Ogden and San Francisco, and Los Angeles and San Francisco, the mails were completely obstructed, and that the strikers refused to permit trains to which Pullman cars were attached to run over the lines mentioned. Thereupon Attorney-General Olney immediately sent the following telegraphic despatch to the United States district attorneys in the State of California:

Washington, D. C.
June 28, 1894.
See that the passage of regular trains, carrying United States mails in the usual and ordinary way, as contemplated by the act of Congress and directed by the Postmaster-General, is not obstructed. Procure warrants or any other available process from United States courts against any and all persons engaged in such obstructions, and direct the marshal to execute the same by such number of deputies or such posse as may be necessary.

On the same day, and during a number of days immediately following, complaints of a similar character, sometimes accompanied by charges of forcible seizure of trains and other violent disorders, poured in upon the Attorney-General from all parts of the West and Southwest. These complaints came from post-office officials, from United States marshals and district attorneys, from railroad managers, and from other officials and private citizens. In all cases of substantial representation of interference with the carriage of mails, a despatch identical with that already quoted was sent by the Attorney-General to the United States district attorneys in the disturbed localities; and this was supplemented, whenever necessary, by such other prompt action as the different emergencies required.

I shall not enter upon an enumeration of all the disorders and violence, the defiance of law and authority, and the obstructions of national functions and duties, which occurred in many localities as a consequence of this labor contention, thus tremendously reinforced and completely under way. It is my especial purpose to review the action taken by the Government for the maintenance of its own authority and the protection of the interests intrusted to its keeping, so far as they were endangered by this disturbance; and I do not intend to specifically deal with the incidents of the strike except in so far as a reference to them may be necessary to show conditions which not only justified but actually obliged the Government to resort to stern and unusual measures in the assertion of its prerogatives.

Inasmuch, therefore, as the city of Chicago was the birthplace of the disturbance and the home of its activities, and because it was the field of its most pronounced and malign manifestations, as well as the place of its final extinction, I shall meet the needs of my subject if I supplement what has been already said by a recital of events occurring at this central point. . . .

Owing to the enforced relationship of Chicago to the strike which started within its borders, and because of its importance as a center of railway traffic, Government officials at Washington were not surprised by the early and persistent complaints of mail and interstate commerce obstructions which reached them from that city. It was from the first anticipated that this would be the seat of the most serious complications, and the place where the strong arm of the law would be most needed. In these circumstances it would have been a criminal neglect of duty if those charged with the protection of governmental agencies and the enforcement of orderly obedience and submission to Federal authority, had been remiss in preparations for any emergency in that quarter.

On the thirtieth day of June the district attorney at Chicago reported by telegraph that mail trains in the suburbs of Chicago were, on the previous night, stopped by strikers, that an engine had been cut off and disabled, and that conditions were growing more and more likely to culminate in the stoppage of all trains; and he recommended that the marshal be authorized to employ a force of special deputies who should be placed on trains to protect mails and detect the parties guilty of such interference. In reply to this despatch Attorney-General

Olney on the same day authorized the marshal to employ additional deputies as suggested, and designated Edwin Walker, an able and prominent attorney in Chicago, as special counsel for the Government, to assist the district attorney in any legal proceedings that might be instituted. He also notified the district attorney of the steps thus taken, and enjoined upon him that "action ought to be prompt and vigorous," and also directed him to confer with the special counsel who had been employed. In a letter of the same date addressed to this special counsel, the Attorney-General, in making suggestions concerning legal proceedings, wrote: "It has seemed to me that if the rights of the United States were vigorously asserted in Chicago, the origin and center of the demonstration, the result would be to make it a failure everywhere else, and to prevent its spread over the entire country"; and in that connection he indicated that it might be advisable, instead of relying entirely upon warrants issued under criminal statutes against persons actually guilty of the offense of obstructing United States mails, to apply to the courts for injunctions which would restrain and prevent any attempt to commit such offense. This suggestion contemplated the inauguration of legal proceedings in a regular and usual way to restrain those prominently concerned in the interference with the mails and the obstruction of interstate commerce, basing such proceedings on the proposition that, under the Constitution and laws, these subjects were in the exclusive care of the Government of the United States, and that for their protection the Federal courts were competent under general principles of law to intervene by injunction; and on the further ground that under an act of Congress, passed July 2, 1890, conspiracies in restraint of trade or commerce among the several States were declared to be illegal, and the circuit courts of the United States were therein expressly given jurisdiction to prevent and restrain such conspiracies.

On the first day of July the district attorney reported to the Attorney-General that he was preparing a bill of complaint to be presented to the court the next day, on an application for an injunction. He further reported that very little mail and no freight was moving, that the marshal was using all his force to prevent riots and the obstruction of tracks, and that this force was clearly inadequate. On the same day the marshal reported that the situation was desperate, that he had sworn in over four hundred deputies, that many more would be required to protect mail trains, and that he expected great trouble the next day. He further expressed the opinion that one hundred riot guns were needed.

Upon the receipt of these reports, and anticipating an attempt to serve injunctions on the following day, the Attorney-General immediately sent a despatch to the district attorney directing him to report at once if the process of the court should be resisted by such force as the marshal could not overcome, and suggesting that the United States judge should join in such report. He at the same time sent a despatch to the special counsel requesting him to report his view of the situation as early as the forenoon of the next day.

In explanation of these two despatches it should here be said that the desperate character of this disturbance was not in the least under estimated by executive officials at Washington; and it must be borne in mind that while menacing conditions were moving swiftly and accumulating at Chicago, like conditions, inspired and supported from that central point, existed in many other places within the area of the strike's contagion.

Of course it was hoped by those charged with the responsibility of dealing with the situation, that a direct assertion of authority by the marshal and a resort to the restraining power of the courts would prove sufficient for the emergency. Notwithstanding, however, an anxious desire to avoid measures more radical, the fact had not been overlooked that a contingency might occur which would compel a resort to military force. The key to these despatches of the Attorney-General is found in the determination of the Federal authorities to overcome by any lawful and constitutional means all resistance to governmental functions as related to the transportation of mails, the operation of interstate commerce, and the preservation of the property of the United States.

The Constitution requires that the United States shall protect each of the States against invasion, "and on application of the legislature, or of the executive (when the legislature cannot be convened), against domestic violence." There was plenty of domestic violence in the city of Chicago and in the State of Illinois during the early days of July, 1894; but no application was made to the Federal government for assistance. It was probably a very fortunate circumstance that the presence of United States soldiers in Chicago at that time did not depend upon the request or desire of Governor Altgeld.

Section 5298 of the Revised Statutes of the United States provides: "Whenever, by reason of unlawful obstructions, combinations or assemblages of persons, or rebellion against the authority of the United States, it shall become impracticable in the judgment of the President to enforce, by the ordinary course of judicial proceedings, the laws of the United States within any State or Territory, it shall be lawful for the President to call forth the militia of any or all of the States, and to employ such parts of the land or naval forces of the United States as he may deem necessary to enforce the faithful execution of the laws of the United States, or to suppress such rebellion, in whatever State or Territory thereof the laws of the United States may be forcibly opposed, or the execution thereof be forcibly obstructed"; and section 5299 provides: "Whenever any insurrection, domestic violence, unlawful combinations or conspiracies in any State . . . opposes or obstructs the laws of the United States, or the due execution thereof, or impedes or obstructs the due course of justice under the same, it shall be lawful for the President, and it shall be his duty, to take such measures, by the employment of the militia, or the land and naval forces of the United States, or of either, or by other means as he may deem necessary, for the suppression of such insurrection, domestic violence or combinations."

It was the intention of the Attorney-General to suggest in these despatches that immediate and authoritative information should be given to the Washington authorities if a time should arrive when, under the sanction of general executive authority, or the constitutional and statutory provisions above quoted, a military force would be necessary at the scene of disturbance.

On the 2d of July, the day after these despatches were sent, information was received from the district attorney and special counsel that a sweeping injunction had been granted against Eugene V. Debs, president of the American Railway Union, and other officials of that organization, together with parties whose names were unknown, and that the writs would be served that afternoon. The special counsel also expressed the opinion that it would require Government troops to enforce the orders of the court and protect the transportation of mails.

Major-General Schofield was then in command of the army; and, after a consultation with him, in which the Attorney-General and the Secretary of War took part, I directed the issuance of the following order by telegraph to General Nelson A. Miles, in command of the Military Department of Missouri, with headquarters at Chicago:

> Headquarters of the Army,
> Washington, July 2, 1894.
>
> *To the Commanding-General,*
> *Department of Missouri,*
> *Chicago, Ill.*
>
> You will please make all necessary arrangements confidentially for the transportation of the entire garrison at Fort Sheridan — infantry, cavalry, and artillery — to the lake front in the city of Chicago. To avoid possible interruption of the movement by rail and by marching through a part of the city, it may be advisable to bring them by steam-boat. Please consider this matter and have the arrangements perfected without delay. You may expect orders at any time for the movement. Acknowledge receipt and report in what manner movement is to be made.
>
> J. M. SCHOFIELD,
> *Major-General Commanding.*

It should by no means be inferred from this despatch that it had been definitely determined that the use of a military force was inevitable. It was still hoped that the effect of the injunction would be such that this alternative might be avoided. A painful emergency is created when public duty forces the necessity of placing trained soldiers face to face with riotous opposition to the general Government, and an acute and determined defiance to law and order. This course, once entered upon, admits of no backward step; and an appreciation of the consequences that may ensue cannot fail to oppress those responsible for its adoption with sadly disturbing reflections. Nevertheless, it was perfectly plain that, whatever the outcome might be, the situation positively demanded such precaution and preparation as would insure readiness and promptness in case the presence of a military force should finally be found necessary.

On the morning of the next day, July 3, the Attorney-General received a letter from Mr. Walker, the special counsel, in which, after referring to the issuance of the injunctions and setting forth that the marshal was engaged in serving them, he wrote:

I do not believe that the marshal and his deputies can protect the railroad companies in moving their trains, either freight or passenger, including, of course, the trains carrying United States mails. Possibly, however, the service of the writ of injunction will have a restraining influence upon Debs and other officers of the association. If it does not, from present appearances, I think it is the opinion of all that the orders of the court cannot be enforced except by the aid of the regular army.

Thereupon the Attorney-General immediately sent this despatch to the district attorney:

I trust use of United States troops will not be necessary. If it becomes necessary, they will be used promptly and decisively upon the justifying facts being certified to me. In such case, if practicable, let Walker and the marshal and United States judge join in statement as to the exigency.

A few hours afterward the following

urgent and decisive despatch from the marshal, endorsed by a judge of the United States court and the district attorney and special counsel, was received by the Attorney-General.

Chicago, Ill., July 3, 1894.
Hon. Richard Olney, *Attorney-General*
Washington, D. C.:

When the injunction was granted yesterday, a mob of from two to three thousand held possession of a point in the city near the crossing of the Rock Island by other roads, where they had already ditched a mail-train, and prevented the passing of any trains, whether mail or otherwise. I read the injunction writ to this mob and commanded them to disperse. The reading of the writ met with no response except jeers and hoots. Shortly after, the mob threw a number of baggage-cars across the track, since when no mail-train has been able to move. I am unable to disperse the mob, clear the tracks, or arrest the men who were engaged in the acts named, and believe that no force less than the regular troops of the United States can procure the passage of the mail trains, or enforce the orders of the courts. I believe people engaged in trades are quitting employment to-day, and in my opinion will be joining the mob to-night and especially to-morrow; and it is my judgment that the troops should be here at the earliest moment. An emergency has arisen for their presence in this city.
J. W. ARNOLD,
United States Marshal.

We have read the foregoing, and from that information, and other information that has come to us, believe that an emergency exists for the immediate presence of United States troops.
P. S. GROSSCUP, *Judge*
EDWIN WALKER   } *Attys.*
THOMAS E. MILCHRIST }

In the afternoon of the same day the following order was telegraphed from army headquarters in the city of Washington:

War Department,
Headquarters of the Army.
Washington, D. C., July 3, 1894.
4 o'clock P.M.

To Martin, *Adjutant-General,*
Headquarters Department of Missouri,
Chicago, Ill.

It having become impracticable in the judgment of the President to enforce by the ordinary course of judicial proceedings the laws of the United States, you will direct Colonel Crofton to move his entire command at once to the city of Chicago (leaving the necessary guard at Fort Sheridan), there to execute the orders and processes of the United States court, to prevent the obstruction of the United States mails, and generally to enforce the faithful execution of the laws of the United States. He will confer with the United States marshal, the United States district attorney, and Edwin Walker, special counsel. Acknowledge receipt and report action promptly. By order of the President.

J. M. SCHOFIELD, *Major-General.*

Immediately after this order was issued, the following despatch was sent to the district attorney by the Attorney-General:

Colonel Crofton's command ordered to Chicago by the President. As to disposition and movement of troops, yourself, Walker, and marshal should confer with Colonel Crofton and with Colonel Martin, adjutant-general at Chicago. While action should be prompt and decisive, it should of course be kept within the limits provided by the Constitution and laws. Rely upon yourself and Walker to see that this is done.

Colonel Martin, adjutant-general at Chicago, reported, the same night at half-past nine o'clock, that the order for the movement of troops was, immediately on its receipt by him, transmitted to Fort Sheridan, and that Colonel Crofton's command started for Chicago at nine o'clock.

During the forenoon of the next day,

July 4, Colonel Martin advised the War Department that Colonel Crofton reported his command in the city of Chicago at 10:15 that morning. After referring to the manner in which the troops had been distributed, this officer added: "People seem to feel easier since arrival of troops."

General Miles, commanding the department, arrived in Chicago the same morning, and at once assumed direction of military movements. In the afternoon of that day he sent a report to the War Department at Washington, giving an account of the disposition of troops, recounting an unfavorable condition of affairs, and recommending an increase of the garrison at Fort Sheridan sufficient to meet any emergency.

In response to this despatch General Miles was immediately authorized to order six companies of infantry from Fort Leavenworth, in Kansas, and two companies from Fort Brady, in Michigan, to Fort Sheridan.

On the fifth day of July he reported that a mob of over two thousand had gathered that morning at the stock-yards, crowded among the troops, obstructed the movement of trains, knocked down a railroad official, and overturned about twenty freight-cars, which obstructed all freight and passenger traffic in the vicinity of the stock-yards, and that the mob had also derailed a passenger-train on the Pittsburg, Fort Wayne and Chicago Railroad, and burned switches. To this recital of violent demonstrations he added the following statement:

The injunction of the United States court is openly defied, and unless the mobs are dispersed by the action of the police or they are fired upon by United States troops, more serious trouble may be expected, as the mob is increasing and becoming more defiant.

In view of the situation as reported by General Miles, a despatch was sent to him by General Schofield directing him to concentrate his troops in order that they might act more effectively in the execution of orders theretofore given, and in the protection of United States property. This despatch concluded as follows:

The mere preservation of peace and good order in the city is, of course, the province of the city and state authorities.

The situation on the sixth day of July was thus described in a despatch sent in the afternoon of that day by General Miles to the Secretary of War:

In answer to your telegram, I report the following: Mayor Hopkins last night issued a proclamation prohibiting riotous assemblies and directing the police to stop people from molesting railway communication. Governor Altgeld has ordered General Wheeler's brigade on duty in Chicago to support the Mayor's authority. So far, there have been no large mobs like the one of yesterday, which moved from 51st Street to 18th Street before it dispersed. The lawlessness has been along the line of the railways, destroying and burning more than one hundred cars and railway buildings, and obstructing transportation in various ways, even to the extent of cutting telegraph lines. United States troops have dispersed mobs at 51st Street, Kensington, and a company of infantry is moving along the Rock Island to support a body of United States marshals in making arrests for violating the injunction of the United States court. Of the twenty-three roads centering in Chicago, only six are unobstructed in freight, passenger, and mail transportation. Thirteen are at present entirely obstructed, and ten are running only mail- and passenger-trains. Large numbers of trains moving in and out of the city have been stoned and fired upon by mobs, and one engineer killed. There was a secret meeting to-day of Debs and the representatives of labor unions considering the advisability of a general strike of all labor unions. About one hundred men were present at that meeting. The result is not yet known. United States troops are at the stock-yards, Kensington, Blue Island, crossing of 51st Street, and have been moving along some of the lines: the balance, eight companies of infantry, battery of artillery, and one troop of cavalry, are camped on Lake Front Park, ready for any emergency and to protect Government buildings and property. It is learned from the Fire Department, City Hall, that a party of strikers has been going through the vicinity from 14th to 41st streets and Stewart Avenue freight-yards, throwing gasoline on freight-cars all through that section. Captain Ford, of the Fire Department, was badly stoned this morning. Troops have just dispersed a mob of incendiaries on Fort Wayne tracks, near 51st Street, and fires that were started have been suppressed. Mob just captured mail-train at 47th Street, and troops sent to disperse them.

On the eighth day of July, in view of the apparently near approach of a crisis which the Government had attempted to avoid, the following Executive Proclamation was issued and at once extensively published in the city of Chicago:

Whereas, by reason of unlawful obstruction, combinations and assemblages of persons, it has become impracticable, in the judgment of the President, to enforce, by the ordinary course of judicial proceedings, the laws of the United States within the State of Illinois, and especially in the city of Chicago within said State; and

Whereas, for the purpose of enforcing the faithful execution of the laws of the United States and protecting its property and removing obstructions to the United States mails in the State and city aforesaid, the President has employed a part of the military forces of the United States: —

Now, therefore, I, Grover Cleveland, President of the United States, do hereby admonish all good citizens, and all persons who may be or may come within the city and State aforesaid, against aiding, countenancing, encouraging, or taking any part in such unlawful obstructions, combinations, and assemblages; and I hereby warn all persons engaged in or in any way connected with such unlawful obstructions, combinations, and assemblages to disperse and retire peaceably to their respective abodes on or before twelve o'clock noon of the 9th day of July instant.

Those who disregard this warning and persist in taking part with a riotous mob in forcibly resisting and obstructing the execution of the laws of the United States, or interfering with the functions of the Government, or destroying or attempting to destroy the property belonging to the United States or under its protection, cannot be regarded otherwise than as public enemies.

Troops employed against such a riotous mob will act with all the moderation and forbearance consistent with the accomplishment of the desired end; but the stern necessities that confront them will not with certainty permit discrimination between guilty participants and those who are mingling with them from curiosity and without criminal intent. The only safe course, therefore, for those not actually participating, is to abide at their homes, or at least not to be found in the neighborhood of riotous assemblages.

While there will be no vacillation in the decisive treatment of the guilty, this warning is especially intended to protect and save the innocent.

On the 10th of July, Eugene V. Debs, the president of the American Railway Union, together with its vice-president, general secretary, and one other who was an active director, were arrested upon indictments found against them for complicity in the obstruction of mails and interstate commerce. Three days afterward our special counsel expressed the opinion that the strike was practically broken. . . .

On the seventeenth day of July an information was filed in the United States Circuit Court at Chicago against Debs and the three other officials of the Railway Union who had been arrested on indictment a few days before, but were then at large on bail. This information alleged that these parties had been guilty of open, continued, and defiant disobedience of the injunction which was served on them July 3, forbidding them to do certain specified acts tending to incite and aid the obstruction of the carriage of mails and the operation of interstate commerce. On the footing of this information these parties were brought before the court to show cause why they should not be punished for contempt in disobeying the injunction. Instead of giving bail for their freedom pending the investigation of this charge against them, as they were invited to do, they preferred to be committed to custody — perhaps intending by such an act of martyrdom either to revive a waning cause, or to gain a plausible and justifying excuse for the collapse of their already foredoomed movement. Debs himself, in speaking of this event afterward, said: "As soon as the employees found that we were arrested and taken from the scene of action they became demoralized, and that ended the strike."

That the strike ended about the time of this second arrest is undoubtedly true; for, during the few days immediately preceding and following the seventeenth day of July, reports came from nearly all the localities to which the strike had spread, indicating its defeat and the accomplishment of all the purposes of the Government's interference. . . .

I hope I have been successful thus far in my effort satisfactorily to exhibit the extensive reach and perilous tendency of the convulsion under consideration, the careful promptness which characterized the interference of the Government, the constant desire of the national administration to avoid extreme measures, the scrupulous limitation of its interference to purposes which were clearly within its constitutional competency and duty, and the gratifying and important results of its conservative but stern activity.

I must not fail to mention here as part of the history of this perplexing affair, a contribution made by the governor of Illinois to its annoyances. This official not only refused to regard the riotous disturbances within the borders of his State as a sufficient cause for an application to the Federal Government for its protection "against domestic violence" under the mandate of the Constitution, but he actually protested against the presence of Federal troops sent into the State upon the general Government's own initiative and for the purpose of defending itself in the exercise of its well-defined legitimate functions. . . .

I shall conclude the treatment of my subject by a brief reference to the legal proceedings which grew out of this disturbance, and finally led to an adjudication by the highest court in our land, establishing in an absolutely authoritative manner and for all time the power of the national Government to protect itself in the exercise of its functions.

It will be recalled that in the course of our narrative we left Mr. Debs, the president of the Railway Union, and his three associates in custody of the law, on the seventeenth day of July, awaiting an investigation of the charge of contempt of court made against them, based upon their disobedience of the writs of injunction forbidding them to do certain things in aid or encouragement of interference with mail transportation or interstate commerce.

This investigation was so long delayed that the decision of the Circuit Court before which the proceedings were pending was not rendered until the fourteenth day of December, 1894. On that date the court delivered an able and carefully considered decision finding Debs and his associates guilty of contempt of court, basing its decision upon the provisions of the law of Congress, passed in 1890, entitled: "An act to protect trade and commerce against unlawful restraint and monopolies"; sometimes called the Sherman Anti-Trust Law. Thereupon the parties were sentenced on said conviction to confinement in the county jail for terms varying from three to six months.

Afterward, and on the 14th day of January, 1895, the prisoners applied to the Supreme Court of the United States for a writ of habeas corpus to relieve them from imprisonment, on the ground that the facts found against them by the Circuit Court did not constitute disobedience of the writs of injunction and that their commitment in the manner and for the reasons alleged was without justification and not within the constitutional power and jurisdiction of that tribunal.

On this application, the case was elaborately argued before the Supreme Court in March, 1895; and on the twenty-seventh day of May, 1895, the court rendered its decision, upholding on the broadest grounds the proceedings of the Circuit Court and confirming its adjudication and the commitment to jail of the petitioners thereupon. . . .

Thus the Supreme Court of the United States has written the closing words of this history, tragical in many of its details, and in every line provoking sober reflection. As we gratefully turn its concluding page, those who were most nearly related by executive responsibility to the troublous days whose story is told may well especially congratulate themselves on the part which fell to them in marking out the way and clearing the path, now unchangeably established, which shall hereafter guide our nation safely and surely in the exercise of the important functions which represent the people's trust. . . .

Eugene V. Debs: THE FEDERAL GOVERNMENT AND THE CHICAGO STRIKE

IN the July issue of *McClure's Magazine* ex-President Grover Cleveland has an article on "The Government in the Chicago Strike of 1894." That there may be no mistake about the meaning of "government" in this connection it should be understood that Mr. Cleveland has reference to the Federal government, of which he was the executive head at the time of the strike in question, and not to the State government of Illinois, or the municipal government of Chicago, both of which were overridden and set at defiance by the executive authority, enforced by the military power of the Federal government under the administration of Mr. Cleveland.

CLEVELAND VINDICATES HIMSELF

The ex-President's article not only triumphantly vindicates his administration but congratulates its author upon the eminent service he rendered the republic in a critical hour when a labor strike jarred its foundations and threatened its overthrow.

It may be sheer coincidence that Mr. Cleveland's eulogy upon his patriotic administration and upon himself as its central and commanding figure appears on the eve of a national convention composed largely of his disciples, who are urging his fourth nomination for the presidency for the very reasons set forth in the article on the Chicago strike.

However this may be, it is certain that of his own knowledge ex-President Cleveland knows nothing of the strike he discusses; that the evidence upon which he acted officially and upon which he now bases his conclusion was *ex parte*, obtained wholly from the railroad interests and those who represented or were controlled by these interests, and it is not strange, therefore, that he falls into a series of errors beginning with the cause of the disturbance and running all through his account of it, as may be proved beyond doubt by reference to the "Report on the Chicago Strike" by the "United States Strike Commission" of his own appointment.

WHAT WAS THE CHICAGO STRIKE?

Simply one of the many battles that have been fought and are yet to be fought in the economic war between capital and labor. Pittsburg, Homestead, Buffalo, Latimer, Pana, Coeur d'Alene, Cripple Creek and Telluride recall a few of the battles fought in this country in the world-wide struggle for industrial emancipation. . . .

THE OBJECT OF FEDERAL INTERFERENCE

From the Federal Judge who sat on the bench as the protégé of the late George M. Pullman to whose influence he was indebted for his appointment – as he was to the railroad companies for the

Excerpted from: *Debs: His Life, Writings and Speeches* (Chicago: Charles H. Kerr & Company Co-Operative, 1908), pp. 181–205. (Copyrighted 1908 by The Appeal to Reason.)

annual passes he had in his pocket — down to the last thug sworn in by the railroads and paid by the railroads (p. 340 report of Strike Commission) to serve the railroads as United States deputy marshal, the one object of the Federal Court and its officers was, not the enforcement of law and preservation of order, but the breaking up of the strike in the interest of the railroad corporations, and it was because of this fact that John P. Altgeld, Governor of Illinois, and John P. Hopkins, Mayor of Chicago, were not in harmony with President Cleveland's administration and protested against the Federal troops being used in their state and city for such a malign purpose.

This is the fact and I shall prove it beyond doubt before this article is concluded. . . .

THE CAUSE OF THE PULLMAN STRIKE

It is easy for Mr. Cleveland and others who were on the side of the railroads to introduce copies of documents, reports, etc., for the simple reason that the Federal Court at Chicago compelled the telegraph companies to deliver up copies of all our telegrams and copies of the proceedings of the convention and other meetings of the American Railway Union, including secret sessions, but the Federal Court did not call upon the railroads to produce the telegrams that passed among themselves, nor between their counsel and the Federal authorities, nor the printed proceedings of the General Managers' Association for public inspection and as a basis for criminal prosecution.

HAD THE STRIKE WON

Nevertheless, there is available proof sufficient to make it clear to the unprejudiced mind, to the honest man who seeks the truth, that the United States government, under the administration of President Grover Cleveland, was at the beck and call of the railroad corporations, acting as one through the "General Managers' Association," and that these corporations, with the Federal Courts and troops to back them up, had swarms of mercenaries sworn in as deputy marshals to incite violence as a pretext for taking possession of the headquarters of the American Railway Union by armed force, throwing its leaders into prison without trial and breaking down the union that was victorious, maligning, brow-beating and persecuting its peaceable and law-abiding members and putting the railroad corporations in supreme control of the situation.

That was the part of President Cleveland in the Chicago strike, and for this achievement the railroad combine and the trusts in general remember him with profound gratitude, and are not only willing but anxious that he shall be President of the United States forevermore.

A PRECEDENT FOR FUTURE ACTION

In the closing paragraph of his article Mr. Cleveland compliments his administration upon having cleared the way "which shall hereafter guide our nation safely and surely in the exercise of its functions which represent the people's trust." The word "people's" is not only superfluous but mischievous and fatal to the truth. Omit that and the ex-President's statement will not be challenged.

CLEVELAND'S FIRST MOVE

How did President Cleveland begin operations in the Chicago strike? Among the first things he did, as he himself tells us, was to appoint Edwin Walker as special counsel for the government.

Who was Edwin Walker?

"An able and prominent attorney," says Mr. Cleveland.

Is that all?

Not quite. At the time President Cleveland and his Attorney-General, Richard Olney, designated Edwin Walker, upon recommendation of the railroads, as special counsel to the government, for which alleged service he was paid a fee that amounted to a fortune, *the said Edwin Walker was already the counsel for the Chicago, Milwaukee & St. Paul Railway.*

Turning for a moment to "Who's Who in America," we find:

Walker, Edwin, lawyer . . . removed to Chicago in 1865; has represented several railroads as general solicitor since 1860. Illinois counsel for C., M. & St. P. R. R. since 1870; also partner in firm of W. P. Rend & Co., coal miners and shippers. Was counsel for the railway companies and special counsel for the United States in the lawsuits growing out of the great railroad strike of 1894.

THE SIGNIFICANCE OF THE APPOINTMENT

Here is the situation: There is a conflict between the General Managers' Association, representing the railroads, and the American Railway Union, representing the employes. Perfect quiet and order prevail, as I shall show, but the railroads are beaten to a standstill, utterly helpless, cannot even move a mail car, simply because their employes have quit their service and left the premises in a body. Note also that the employes were willing to haul the mail trains and all other trains, refusing only to handle Pullman cars until the Pullman Company should consent to arbitrate its disagreement with its striking and starving employes. But the railroad officials determined that if the Pullman cars were not handled the mail cars should not move.

This is how and why the mails were obstructed and this was the pretext for Federal interference. In a word, President Cleveland, obedient to the railroads, took sides with them and supported them in their conflict with their employes with all the powers of the Federal government.

STRIKE COMMISSION REPORT VS. CLEVELAND

To bear out these facts it is not necessary to go outside of the official report of the Strike Commission, which anyone may verify at his pleasure. . . .

Upon Walker's representations Cleveland acted; upon Walker's demand, the Federal soldiers marched into Chicago; upon Walker's command, the great government of the United States obeyed with all the subserviency of a trained lackey.

SUPPOSE CLEVELAND HAD APPOINTED DARROW?

Suppose that President Cleveland had appointed Clarence S. Darrow, attorney for the American Railway Union, instead of Edwin Walker, attorney of the General Managers' Association, as special counsel for the government!

And suppose that Darrow had ordered the offices of the General Managers' Association sacked, the books, papers and correspondence, including the unopened private letters of the absent officers, packed up and carted away and the offices put under the guard of Federal ruffians, in flagrant violation of the Constitution of the United States, as was done by order of Walker with the offices of the American Railway Union!

And suppose, moreover, that the American Railway Union, backed up by Darrow, agent of the United States government, had sworn in an army of "thugs, thieves and ex-convicts" (see official report of Michael Brennan, superintendent of Chicago police to the Council of Chicago) to serve the American Railway Union as deputy United States marshals and "conservators of peace and order"!

And suppose, finally, that the expected trouble had followed, would anyone in possession of his senses belive that these things had been done to protect life and property and preserve law and order?

That is substantially the case that President Cleveland is trying to make for himself and his administration out of their participation in the Chicago strike.

THE REAL LAWBREAKER THE RAILROADS

The implication that runs through Mr. Cleveland's entire article is that the railway corporations were paragons of peace and patriotism, law and order, while the railway employes were a criminal, desperate and blood-thirsty mob which had to be suppressed by the strong arm of the government.

No wonder the ex-President is so dear to the iron heart of the railroad trust and every other trust that uses the government and its officers and soldiers to further its own sordid ends.

Let us consider for a moment these simple questions:

Who are the more law-abiding, the predatory railroad corporations or the hard-worked railroad employes?

What railroad corporation in the United States lives up to the law of the land? Not one.

What body of railroad employes violates it? Not one.

THE BRAZEN DEFIANCE OF LAW
BY THE RAILROADS

The railroad corporations are notorious for their brazen defiance of every law that is designed to curb their powers or restrain their rapacity.

The railroad corporations have their lobby at Washington and at every State

capital; they bribe legislators, corrupt courts, debauch politics and commit countless other legal and moral crimes against the commonwealth. . . .

THE STRIKE COMMISSION'S REPORT

Now for a few facts about the strike. It began May 11, 1894, and was perfectly peaceable and orderly until the army of "thugs, thieves and ex-convicts," as Superintendent of Police Brennan called them in his official report to the Council of Chicago, were sworn in as deputies by the United States marshal at the command of Edwin Walker, attorney of the General Managers' Association and special counsel to the government. Let us quote the report of the Strike Commission, consisting of Carroll D. Wright, Commissioner of Labor, who served ex-officio; John D. Kernan, of New York, and N. E. Worthington, of Illinois, two lawyers, appointed by President Cleveland.

Let it be noted that the railway employes, that is to say, labor, the working class, had no representative on this Commission.

From the report they issued we quote as follows:

A.R.U. LEADERS ADVISE AGAINST STRIKE

"It is undoubtedly true that the officers and directors of the American Railway Union did not want a strike at Pullman and advised against it. . . . (P. xxvii.) (Yet the people were told over and over and still believe that Debs ordered the strike.)

RAILROADS SET THE EXAMPLE

It should be noted that until the railroads set the example a general union of railroad employes was never attempted. (P. xxxi.)

The refusal of the General Managers' Association to recognize and deal with such a combination of labor as the American Railway Union seems arrogant and absurd when we consider its standing before the law, its assumptions, and its past and obviously contemplated future action. (P. xxxi.)

... The rents (at Pullman) are from 20 to 25 per cent higher than rents in Chicago or surrounding towns for similar accommodations. (P. xxxv.)

STRIKE COMMISSION CONTRADICTS CLEVELAND

The strike occurred on May 11, and from that time until the soldiers went to Pullman, about July 4, 300 strikers were placed about the company's property, professedly to guard it from destruction or interference. This guarding of property in strikes is, as a rule, a mere pretense. Too often the real object of guards is to prevent newcomers from taking the strikers' places, by persuasion, often to be followed, if ineffectual, by intimidation and violence. The Pullman Company claims this was the real object of these guards. *These strikers at Pullman are entitled to be believed to the contrary in this matter, because of their conduct and forbearance after May 11. It is in evidence, and uncontradicted, that no violence or destruction of property by strikers or sympathizers took place at Pullman, and that until July 3* (when the Federal troops came upon the scene) *no extraordinary protection was had from the police and military against even anticipated disorder.* (P. xxxviii.)

This paragraph from the report of Mr. Cleveland's own Commission is sufficient answer to Mr. Cleveland's article. It is conclusive, crushing, overwhelming.

DEPUTIES STARTED THE TROUBLE

There was no trouble at Pullman, nor at Chicago, nor elsewhere, until the railroad-United States deputy marshals were sworn in, followed by the Federal troops.

Governor Altgeld, patriot and statesman, knew it and protested against the troops.

Mayor John P. Hopkins knew it and declared that he was fully competent to preserve the peace of the city.

SUPERINTENDENT OF POLICE CALLED THEM "THUGS"

Michael Brennan, Superintendent of the Chicago police, knew it and denounced the deputy marshals Edwin Arnold's hirelings, the General Managers' Association's incendiaries and sluggers, as "thugs, thieves and ex-convicts."

These were the "gentlemen" President Cleveland's government pressed into service upon requisition of the railroads to preserve order and protect life and property, and this is what the ex-President calls "the power of the National government to protect itself in the exercise of its functions."

As to just what these "functions" are when Grover Cleveland is President, the railroad corporations understand to a nicety and agree to by acclamation.

PROFOUND PEACE RESTORED

The only trouble, when the "deputies" were sworn in, followed by the soldiers, was that there was no trouble. That is the secret of subsequent proceedings. The railroads were paralyzed. Profound peace reigned. The people demanded of the railroads that they operate their trains. They could not do it. Not a man would serve them. They were completely defeated and the banners of organized labor floated triumphant in the breeze.

Beaten at every point, their schemes all frustrated, outgeneraled in tactics and strategy, the corporations played their trump card by an appeal to the Federal judiciary and the Federal administration. To this appeal the response came quick as lightning from a storm cloud.

PEACE FATAL TO MANAGERS' ASSOCIATION

Peace and order were fatal to the railroad corporations. Violence was as necessary to them as peace was to the employes. They realized that victory could only be snatched from labor by an appeal to violence in the name of peace.

First, deputy marshals. The very day they were appointed the trouble began. The files of every Chicago paper prove it. The report of the Strike Commission does the same.

That was what they were hired for and their character is sufficient evidence of their guilt.

Second, fires (but no Pullman palace cars were lighted) and riots (but no strikers were implicated).

Third, the capitalist-owned newspapers and Associated Press flashed the news over all the wires that the people were at the mercy of a mob and that the strikers were burning and sacking the city.

Fourth, the people (especially those at a distance who knew nothing except what they saw in the papers) united in the frenzied cry: "Down with anarchy! Down with the A. R. U.! Death to the strikers!"

DISTURBANCES STARTED BY DEPUTY MARSHALS

The first trouble instigated by the deputy marshals was the signal for the Federal Court injunctions, and they came like a succession of lightning flashes.

Next, the general offices of the American Railway Union were sacked and put under guard and communication destroyed. (Later Judge Grosscup rebuked the Federal satraps who committed this outrageous crime, but he did not pretend to bring them to justice.)

Next, the leaders of the strike were arrested, not for crime, but for alleged violation of an injunction.

Next, they were brought into court, denied trial by jury, pronounced guilty by the same judge who had issued the injunction, and sent to jail for from three to six months.

THE CONCLUDING WORDS NOT YET WRITTEN

The Supreme Court of the United States, consisting wholly of trained and successful corporation lawyers, affirmed the proceeding and President Cleveland says that they have "written the concluding words of this history."

Did the Supreme Court of the United States write the "concluding words" in the history of chattel slavery when it handed down Chief Justice Taney's decision that black men had "no rights that the white man was bound to respect"?

These "concluding words" will but hasten the overthrow of wage slavery as the "concluding words" of the same Supreme Court in 1857 hastened the overthrow of chattel slavery.

The railroad corporations would rather have destroyed their property and seen Chicago perish than see the American Railway Union triumphant in as noble a cause as ever prompted sympathetic, manly men to action in this world.

PEACE OVERTURES TURNED DOWN

The late Mayor Pingree of Detroit came to Chicago with telegrams from the mayors of over fifty of the largest cities urging that there should be arbitration. (P. xxxix, Report of Strike Commission.) He was turned down without ceremony, and afterwards declared that the railroads were the only criminals and that they were responsible for all the consequences.

June 22, four days before the strike against the railroads, or, rather, the boycott of Pullman cars, took effect, there was a joint meeting of the railroad and Pullman officials. (P. xlii, Report of Strike Commission.) At this meeting it was resolved to defeat the strikers, wipe out the American Railway Union, and, to use their exact words, "that we act unitedly to that end."

This was the only joint meeting of the kind that had ever been held between the officials of the railroad companies and the Pullman company. They mutually determined to stand together to defeat the strike and destroy the union.

Now, to show what regard these gentlemen have for courts and law and morals, this incident will suffice:

RAILWAY OFFICIALS PERJURE THEMSELVES

When the officers of the American Railway Union were indicted by a special and packed grand jury and placed on trial for conspiracy, the general managers of the railroads were put on the witness stand to testify as to what action had been taken at the joint railroad and Pullman meeting described, and each and every one of them perjured himself by swearing that he had no recollection of what had taken place at that meeting. Sitting within a few feet of them I saw their faces turn scarlet under the cross-examination, knowing that they were testifying falsely; that the court knew it, and that every one present knew it; but they stuck to their agreement and uniformly failed to remember that they had resolved to stand together, the railroads agreeing to back the Pullman company in defeating their famishing employes, and the Pullman company pledging itself to stand by the railroads in destroying the American Railway Union.

That is what their own record shows they resolved to do, and a little later they concluded to forget all about it, and to

this they swore in a Federal Court of law.

I have copies of the court record, including the testimony, to prove this, and the files of all the Chicago dailies of that time contain the same testimony.

These are the gentlemen who have so much to say about law and order – the vaunted guardians of morals and good citizenship.

When A. B. Stickney, president of the Chicago Great Western, who had been victimized by them, told them to their faces that there was not an honest official among them and that he would not trust one of them out of his sight, they did not attempt any defense, for they knew that their accuser was on the inside and in position to make good his assertions.

THE DEPUTIES AS VIEWED BY THE
COMMISSION

I must now introduce a little evidence from the report of the Strike Commission bearing upon the United States deputy marshals who were sworn in by the railroads "to protect life and property and preserve the peace":

Page 356: Superintendent Brennan, of the Chicago police, testifies before the Commission that he has a number of deputy marshals in the county jail *arrested while serving the railroads as United States deputy marshals for highway robbery.*

NEWSPAPER REPORTERS' EVIDENCE

Page 370: Ray Stannard Baker, then a reporter for the Chicago *Record*, now on the staff of *McClure's Magazine*, testified as follows in answer to the question as to what he knew of the character of the deputy marshals: "From my experience with them it was very bad. I saw more cases of drunkenness, I believe, among the United States deputy marshals than I did among the strikers.". . .

These were Edwin Walker's justly celebrated guardians of the peace.

Page 370: Harold I. Cleveland, reporter for the Chicago *Herald*, testified: "I was on the tracks of the Western Indiana fourteen days.". . . "I saw in that time a couple of hundred deputy marshals. I think they were a very low, contemptible set of men."

HIRED AND PAID BY THE RAILROADS

Now follows what the Strike Commissioners themselves have to say about the deputy marshals, and their words are specially commended to the thoughtful consideration of their chief, President Cleveland:

United States deputy marshals, to the number of 3,600, were selected by and appointed at request of the General Managers' Association, and of its railroads. They were armed and paid by the railroads, and acted in the double capacity of railroad employes and United States officers. While operating the railroads they assumed and exercised unrestricted United States authority when so ordered by their employers, or whenever they regarded it as necessary. They were not under the direct control of any government official while exercising authority. This is placing officers of the government under control of a combination of railroads. It is a bad precedent, that might well lead to serious consequences.

THE GOVERNMENT SERVES THE CORPORATIONS

Here we have it, upon the authority of President Cleveland's own Commission, that the United States government under his administration furnished the railroad corporations with government officers in the form of deputy marshals to take the places of striking employes, operate the trains and serve in that dual capacity in any way that might be required to crush out the strike. This is perhaps more credit than the ex-President expected to receive. His own Commission charges him, in effect, with serving the railroads as strike-breaker by furnishing government employes to take the places of striking railroad men and arming them with pistols and clubs and with all the authority of government officials.

Page after page bears testimony of the disreputable character of the deputy marshals sworn in to the number of several thousand and turned loose like armed bullies to "preserve the peace."

The report of the Strike Commission contains 681 pages. I have a mass of other testimony, but for the purpose of this article have confined myself to the report of Mr. Cleveland's own Commission.

HOW THE STRIKERS WERE DEFEATED

Hundreds of pages of evidence are given by impartial witnesses to establish the guilt of the railroad corporations, to prove that the leaders of the strike counselled peace and order; that the strikers themselves were law-abiding and used their influence to prevent disorder; that there was no trouble until the murderous deputy marshals were sprung upon the community, and that these instigated trouble to pave the way for injunctions and soldiers and change of public sentiment, thereby defeating the strike.

CONFIRMED BY CLEVELAND

President Cleveland, unwittingly, confirms this fact. On page 232 of his article he quotes approvingly the letter written to Edwin Walker, special counsel of the government and regular counsel of the railroads, by Attorney-General Richard Olney, as follows: "It has seemed to me that if the rights of the United States

(Railroads?) were vigorously asserted in Chicago, the origin and center of the demonstration, the result would be to make it a failure everywhere else, and to prevent its spread over the entire country."

That is the point, precisely the point, and Mr. Cleveland admits it. It is not the "obstruction of the mails," nor disorder, nor the violation of law, that arouses Mr. Cleveland's government and prompts it to "vigorous" assertion of its powers, but the "demonstration," that is, the strike against the railroads; and to put this down, not to move the mails or restore order — a mere pretext which was fully exposed by Governor Altgeld — was the prime cause of Federal interference, and to "make it a failure everywhere" all constitutional restraints were battered down, and as a strike-breaker President Cleveland won imperishable renown.

STRIKE LEADERS EXONERATED
BY THE COMMISSION

Particular attention is invited to the following, which appears on page xlv:

There is no evidence before the Commission that the officers of the American Railway Union at any time participated in or advised intimidation, violence or destruction of property. *They knew and fully appreciated that as soon as mobs ruled the organized forces of society would crush the mobs and all responsible for them in the remotest degree, and that this means defeat.*

And yet they all served prison sentences. Will President Cleveland please explain why? And why they were refused a trial?

IN WHOSE INTERESTS WERE CRIMES
COMMITTED?

Read the above paragraph from the report of the Strike Commission and then answer these questions:

To whose interest was it to have riots and fires, lawlessness and crime?

To whose advantage was it to have disreputable "deputies" do these things?

Why were only freight cars, largely hospital wrecks, set on fire?

Why have the railroads not yet recovered damages from Cook county, Illinois, for failing to protect their property? Why are they so modest and patient with their suits?

The riots and incendiarism turned defeat into victory for the railroads. They could have won in no other way. They had everything to gain and the strikers everything to lose.

The violence was instigated in spite of the strikers, and the report of the Commission proves that they made every effort in their power to preserve the peace.

When a crime is committed in the dark the person who is supposed to be benefitted by it is sought out as the probable culprit, but we are not required to rely upon presumption in this case, for the testimony against the railroads is too clear and complete and convincing to admit of doubt.

IMPRISONED WITHOUT TRIAL

If the crimes committed during the Chicago strike were chargeable to the strikers, why were they not prosecuted? If not, why were they sentenced to prison?

The fact that they were flung into prison without evidence and without trial, and the fact that the Supreme Court affirmed the outrage, seemed to afford Mr. Cleveland special satisfaction, and he accepts what he calls the "concluding words" of the court as his own final vindication.

JUDGE TRUMBULL'S OPINION

The late Senator and Judge Lyman Trumbull, for many years United States Senator, chairman of the Senate Committee on Judiciary, Supreme Judge of Illinois, author of the thirteenth amendment to the Constitution of the United States, personal friend of Abraham Lincoln, and, above all, an honest man, wrote: "The doctrine announced by the Supreme Court in the Debs case places every citizen at the mercy of any prejudiced or malicious Federal judge who may think proper to imprison him."

President Cleveland doubtless understands the import of these ominous words. Let the people, the working people, whom the ex-President regards merely as a mob to be suppressed when they peaceably protest against injustice — let them contemplate these words at their leisure.

When the strike was at its height and the railroads were defeated at every turn, the Federal Court hastily impaneled a special grand jury to indict the strikers. . . .

The jury was impaneled, not to investigate, but to indict.

A *Tribune* reporter, who refused to verify a false interview before the jury, and thereby perjure himself to incriminate the writer, was discharged. The Chicago *Times* published the particulars.

An indictment was speedily returned. "To the penitentiary," was the cry of the railroads and their henchmen. A trial jury was impaneled. Not a juror was accepted who was of the same political party as the defendants. Every possible effort was made to rush the strike leaders to the State prison.

THE FAILURE OF THE PROSECUTION

After all the evidence of the prosecution had been presented they realized that they had miserably failed. Not one particle of incriminating testimony could the railroads produce with all the sleuth hounds they had at their command.

Next came our turn. The General Managers were dumbfounded when they were, one after the other, put on the stand. Eighty-six witnesses were in court to testify as to the riots and fires. Assistant Chief Palmer and other members of the Fire Department were on hand to testify that when they were trying to extinguish the flames in the railroad yards they caught men in the act of cutting the hose and that these men wore the badges of deputy marshals. Other witnesses were policemen who were ready to testify that they had caught these same deputies instigating violence and acts of incendiarism.

THE JURY DUMBFOUNDED

The jury had been packed to convict. When our evidence began to come in their eyes fairly bulged with astonishment. There was a perfect transformation scene. The jurors realized that they had been steeped in prejudice and grossly deceived.

The General Managers testified that they did not remember what had taken place at the joint General Managers' and Pullman meeting. Their printed proceedings were called for. They looked appealingly to Edwin Walker. The terror that overspread their features can never be forgotten by those who witnessed it. Their own printed proceedings would expose their mendacity and convict them of conspiracy and crime. Something must be done, and done quickly. Court adjourned for lunch. When it reconvened Judge Grosscup gravely announced that a juror had been suddenly taken ill and that the trial could not proceed.

THE "ILLNESS" OF A JUROR

The next day and the next the same announcement was repeated. We offered to proceed in any of the several ways provided in such exigencies. The prosecution objected. The cry "To the penitentiary" had subsided. "To let go" was now the order of the railroads. Not another session of court must be held, for their printed proceedings, the private property in the strong box of each member, and full of matter that would convict them, would have to be produced. All the proceedings of the American Railway Union had been produced in evidence by order of the court and the court could not refuse to command the railroad officials to produce the proceedings of their association. These proceedings were brought in at the closing session of the trial, but by order of the court the defendants were forbidden to look into them, and Edwin Walker, the government counsel, watched them with the faithful eye of a trusted guardian.

We were not allowed to examine the proceedings of the General Managers' Association, notwithstanding our proceedings, telegrams, letters and other private communications had been brought into court by order of the judge, inspected by Edwin Walker and others, and printed in the court records for public inspection.

It was at this point that the court adjourned and the juror was taken "ill."

Ten years have elapsed. He is still "ill," and we are still waiting for the court to reconvene and the trial to proceed.

GOVERNMENT REFUSED TO GO ON WITH THE CASE

Every proposition to continue the case was fiercely resisted by Edwin Walker, special counsel of the government and general counsel of the railroads.

Clarence S. Darrow objected to Mr. Walker's appearing in that dual capacity, representing at the same time the government and the railroads — the supposed justice of the one and the vengeful spirit of the other — but Judge Grosscup overruled the objection.

The trial was postponed again and again, the interest in it gradually subsiding, and many months afterward, when it was almost forgotten, the case was quietly stricken from the docket.

JURORS GREET DEFENDANTS

When the remaining eleven jurors were discharged by the court, Edwin Walker extended his hand to them, but they rushed by him and surrounded the writer and his co-defendants, grasping their hands and assuring them, each and every one of them, that they were convinced of their innocence and only regretted that they had been prevented from returning their verdict accordingly. The details appear in the Chicago papers of that time.

At the very time we were being tried for conspiracy we were serving a sentence in prison for contempt, the program being that six months in jail should be followed by as many years in penitentiary.

For a jury to pronounce us innocent in substantially the same case for which we were already serving a sentence would mean not only our complete vindication, but the exposure of the Federal Court that had, at the behest of the railroads, sentenced us to prison without a trial.

And so the trial was abruptly terminated on account of the alleged illness of a juror and they could find no other to take his place. . . .

THE GREATEST INDUSTRIAL BATTLE IN HISTORY

The Chicago strike was in many respects the grandest industrial battle in history, and I am prouder of my small share in it than of any other act of my life.

Men, women and children were on the verge of starvation at the "model city" of Pullman. They had produced the fabulous wealth of the Pullman corporation, but they, poor souls, were compelled to suffer the torment of hunger pangs in the very midst of the abundance their labor had created.

A hundred and fifty thousand railroad employes, their fellow members in the American Railway Union, sympathized with them, shared their earnings with them, and after trying in every peaceable way they could conceive of to touch the flint heart of the Pullman company — every overture being rejected, every suggestion denied, every proposition spurned with contempt — they determined not to pollute their hands and dishonor their manhood by handling Pullman cars and contributing to the suffering and sorrow of their brethren and their wives and babes. And rather than do this they laid down their tools in a body, sacrificed their situations and submitted to persecution, exile and the blacklist; to idleness, poverty, crusts and rags, and I shall love and honor these moral heroes to my latest breath.

There was more of human sympathy, of the essence of brotherhood, of the spirit of real Christianity in this act than in all the hollow pretenses and heartless prayers of those disciples of mammon who cried out against it, and this act will shine forth in increasing splendor long after the dollar worshipers have mingled with the dust of oblivion.

Had the carpenter of Nazareth been in Chicago at the time He would have been on the side of the poor, the heavy-laden and sore at heart, and He would have denounced their oppressors and been sent to prison for contempt of court under President Cleveland's administration.

President Cleveland says that we were put down because we had acted in violation of the Sherman Anti-Trust law of 1890. Will he kindly state what other trusts were proceeded against and what capitalists were sentenced to prison during his administration?

A TRIBUTE TO ALTGELD

He waited ten years to cast his aspersions upon the honor of John P. Altgeld, and if that patriotic statesman had not fallen in the service of the people, if he were still here to defend his official acts, it is not probable that the ex-President would have ventured to assail him.

Reluctantly, indeed, do I close without the space to incorporate his burning messages to President Cleveland and at least some extracts from his masterly speech on "Government by Injunction."

His memory requires no defense, but if it did I could speak better for him than for myself. He never truckled to corporate wealth; he did not compromise with his conscience; he was steadfast in his devotion to truth and in his fidelity to right, and he sought with all his strength to serve the people and the people will gratefully remember him as one of the true men, one of the great souls of his sordid age.

The Chicago strike is not yet settled, and its "concluding pages" are YET TO BE WRITTEN.

Henry James: A DEFENSE OF RICHARD OLNEY

AFTER a fruitless attempt to arrange a settlement by negotiation and arbitration, the American Railway Union voted on June 21st that after the 26th its members should refuse to handle trains to which Pullman cars were attached. The avowed intention of this was to compel the railroads to *boycott* the Pullman Company. But no grievance against the roads was stated by the Union and no direct communication was sent to them by its convention.

Today, as we look back, the action of the American Railway Union seems even more astonishing and even less possible to justify than it appeared at the moment. The gist of it was that, in order to help a strike by shop-workers in the town of Pullman, the Union planned to do nothing less than seize the country's transportation system by the throat and inflict more intolerable discomfort on the country than the country could bear. So inherently and essentially violent was this programme that Debs's orders to the members of the Union to refrain from individual acts of violence were reasonably regarded as formalism and mockery. Of course, too, the strike leaders knew that disorders and hoodlumism would attend such a strike as surely as camp-followers attend the march of the best disciplined army. Debs's plan, putting it baldly, was to hit the public rather than the Company, although his purpose was doubtless to draw the public's attention to the injustices of the Pullman situation and thus induce their removal. His error lay in not seeing that such methods were certain to focus criticism and bitter hostility against his own union. One of the "foolishest" as well as one of the "kindest"

of men is what a sympathetic writer once called him. Surely one of the foolishest! "When you say *strike* you mean *boycott* in this case," said Carroll D. Wright, and Debs replied with the candor which partly accounts for his personal magnetism, "Well, I do not exactly like the term *boycott*. It is a term I do not often use. There is a deep-seated hostility in this country to the term *boycott*." Yet knowing that, he plunged ahead. There have been strikes and threats of strikes on a greater scale since then, but no strike of comparable magnitude has seemed so brutally oblivious of the interests of the nation, so careless of public opinion, so unmeasured, so surprising and consequently so menacing.

This very quality of the Chicago strike relieved Cleveland and Olney of the need of elucidating the issues or "making" public opinion in any way. It forced them to act without any reference to the merits of the dispute at the town of Pullman, and made it obvious that they were not attempting to pass upon such questions. "It is not germane," said Olney, "to consider the origin or the merits of the labor disturbance"; and neither at the moment nor later did he ever express his own opinion about them. He and the President had merely to protect the United States mails promptly, vigorously, and without preliminary proclamations or self-justifying explanations of any kind, and could dispense with all discussion of the strikers' claims. Debs had done for them the work of putting the country in the mood for just that. The boycott which he attempted to establish was so impudent a challenge to government that four people out of five realized, as soon as an

Henry James, *Richard Olney and His Public Service* (Boston: Houghton Mifflin Company, 1923), pp. 43–58. Used by permission.

injunction was published and the first troops began to move, that the Administration was doing what had got to be done. Debs himself admitted it all later. "Have you any doubt," he was asked, "that, if public opinion had been directly informed as to the entire situation, the strike would probably have been averted and that you would have succeeded in your just demands?" "I believe that is true," was his reply. . . .

On the 28th of June, two days after the boycott started, the Postmaster-General's Department advised the Department of Justice that the mails were being detained at Chicago, San Francisco, St. Paul, Salt Lake City, Portland, Oregon, and Los Angeles, and asked that steps should be taken to protect them. The following telegram was thereupon dispatched to the United States Attorneys at the places named:

See that the passage of regular trains carrying United States mails in the usual and ordinary way, as contemplated by act of Congress and directed by the Postmaster General, is not obstructed. Procure warrants or other available process from the United States Courts against any and all persons engaged in such obstruction, and direct marshal to execute the same by such number of deputies or such posse as may be necessary.

Thus, as Olney explained in the Memorandum[1], the Department "took measures to put itself in the position which had induced the President to authorize the use of troops as against the Coxey movement." It enlisted the services of Edwin Walker, an able local lawyer, as special counsel for the Government to aid United States District Attorney Milchrist in Chicago, and on June 30th Olney wrote to Walker:

[1] [Memorandum dictated by Olney in 1901 covering his connection with Cleveland's second Administration. ED.]

It has seemed to me that if the rights of the United States were vigorously asserted in Chicago, the origin and center of the demonstration, the result would be to make it a failure everywhere else and to prevent its spread over the entire country. With yourself directing matters for the Government, I am sure all legal remedies will be resorted to that the facts will warrant.

In this connection it has seemed to me advisable not merely to rely on warrants against persons actually guilty of the offense of obstructing United States mails, but to go into a court of equity and secure restraining orders which shall have the effect of preventing any attempt to commit the offense. With that view I sent a telegram to Mr. Milchrist this morning citing some decisions, which I think may probably be availed of in the present exigency.

The Marshal and the District Attorney have wired me about the employment of fifty deputies. I authorized it, of course. But I feel that the true way of dealing with the matter is by a force which is overwhelming and prevents any attempt at resistance. In that particular, however, I must defer to the better judgment of one who is on the spot and familiar with all the facts of the situation. . . .

And the next day he telegraphed to Walker:

Advantages of bill in equity restraining unlawful combinations against operation Federal laws, whether under Interstate-Commerce Law, Act of July 2, 1890, or on general grounds, are obvious and will doubtless be availed of by you, if practicable. Immediate, vigorous measures at center of disturbance immensely important.

Olney also had other reasons for wanting an injunction — the only legal process by which a *prima facie* case against Debs could be judicially set up without delay. "The President might," he said later, "have used the United States troops to prevent interference with the mails and with interstate commerce on his own initiative — without waiting for action by the courts and without justifying the proceeding as taken to enforce judicial decrees. But . . . it is doubtful — at least seemed doubtful to me at the time — whether the President could be induced to move except in support of the judicial tribunals . . . it was unquestionably better to await its (the judiciary's) movements and make them the basis of executive action."

Milchrist and Walker forthwith acted on their instructions and filed a bill in equity in the Attorney-General's name in which they asked for an injunction both on general grounds and to enforce the provisions of the Sherman Anti-Trust Law, and on July 2d Judges Woods and Grosscup issued a sweeping injunction against Debs and other officers of the Railway Union by name, and against "all other persons combining and conspiring with them, and to all other persons whomsoever."

July 3d Olney telegraphed to Milchrist:

Congratulate you upon the legal situation, which is all that could be desired. Trust use of United States troops will not be necessary. If it becomes necessary, they will be used promptly and decisively upon the justifying facts being certified to me. In such case, if practicable, let Walker and Marshal and United States Judge join in statement as to the exigency.

The following dispatch came from Chicago dated the same day:

When the injunction was granted yesterday a mob of from two to three thousand held possession of a point in the city near the crossing of the Rock Island by other roads, where they had already ditched a mail train, and prevented the passing of any trains,

whether mail or otherwise. I read the injunction writ to this mob and commanded them to disperse. The reading of the writ met with no response except jeers and hoots. Shortly after, the mob threw a number of baggage cars across the track, since when no mail trains have been able to move. I am unable to disperse the mob, clear the tracks, or arrest the men who were engaged in the acts named, and believe that no force less than the regular troops of the United States can procure the passage of the mail trains or enforce the orders of the Court. I believe people engaged in trades are quitting employment to-day, and in my opinion will be joining the mob tonight, and especially to-morrow, and it is my judgment that the troops should be here at the earliest moment. An emergency has arisen for their presence in this city.

J. W. Arnold
United States Marshal

We have read the foregoing, and from that information and other information that has come to us believe that an emergency exists for the immediate presence of the United States troops.

P. S. Grosscup, Judge
Edwin Walker ⎱ Attorneys
Thomas E. Milchrist ⎰

As is well remembered, a detachment of regulars immediately moved into the city.

"The whole business had, of course" (said Olney in the Memorandum) "been the subject of much anxious consultation between the President and the Attorney-General, and to some extent with the other members of the Cabinet. The Secretary of War (Lamont) and General Schofield were in constant communication with the President and the Attorney-General, and the Secretary of State (Gresham) — who was a resident in Chicago — was of course very much interested. He was, however, not impressed with the plan pursued by the Department of Justice in the first instance, and doubted whether the bill in equity as filed was not fatally bad because amounting to an attempt to enjoin against the commission of a crime. The President, however, relied upon the Department of Justice, and in the use of the United States troops, was perfectly content to be able to justify himself on the ground that they were employed merely to enforce judicial processes. . . ."

From June 26th, Debs and the other officers and agents of the Union had urged on the strike at every possible point by speeches, telegrams, and personal exhortation. By July 3d they had brought about what Carroll D. Wright, the Chairman of the Special Commission which later reported to the President, described as "a practical insurrection of all the labor employed on the principal railroads radiating from Chicago and some of their affiliated lines . . . whose influences were felt all over the country." They also attempted to induce a sympathetic walkout of all the unionized trades in Chicago; but at this point the American Federation of Labor brought its influence to bear and no general sympathetic strike occurred. The idle and lawless elements, which were especially numerous about Chicago during the year following the World's Fair, seized upon the occasion, however. "Riots, intimidations, assaults, murder, arson, and burglary" attended the boycott. Counting marshals, deputies, militia, and police along with the two thousand regulars the total force which was employed in restoring order amounted to more than fourteen thousand men.

The injunction crippled the activities of Debs and his lieutenants, however. It forbade everything they most needed to do in order to convert their plan into action. It commanded the defendants named

and all persons combining and conspiring with them, and all other persons whomsoever, absolutely to desist and refrain from in any way or manner interfering with, hindering, obstructing or stopping any of the business of any of the following named railroads;

and, after specifying and amplifying in detail and at length, it explicitly enjoined all persons "from ordering, directing, aiding, assisting or abetting in any manner" the acts of interference already forbidden. It was issued in duplicate in the other jurisdictions in which there was trouble, and it threw on the strike organizers a burden of responsibility which was too great for them to carry. Unless they got the injunction dissolved — which they did not even attempt to do — their every command to their striking men was an open defiance of the courts; and, though they tried for a few days to continue defiantly, the telegrams they sent out — often addressed to agents who had been likewise served with an injunction — no longer compelled obedience. "It was not the soldiers that ended the strike," Debs testified at the subsequent inquiry; "it was not the old brotherhoods that ended the strike; it was simply the United States Courts that ended the strike."

Olney wrote to Richard Watson Gilder (September 22, 1897), *a propos* of General Schofield's book, "Forty-Six Years in the Army":

It has therefore occurred to me since I last wrote you that perhaps you would be glad to have a hint how the General's account of the strike impresses me. It impresses me — I am frank to say — unfavorably. From reading it the natural inference is that the army was the sole instrumentality employed to deal with the strike and that the military power of the Government was resorted to at once — from the beginning — and perhaps without sufficient justification.

Such an idea ought not to gain currency — would produce a bad effect generally — and would be most unjust to President Cleveland.

The military arm was invoked with the greatest reluctance — only after all less drastic means had been employed — and only upon the strongest representations of the acuteness of the crisis by those in whose judgment the President had a right to place implicit reliance.

On the 10th of June [July], the grand jury which Milchrist had summoned at the beginning of the trouble indicted Debs and others for obstructing the mails. They were arrested and gave bail. On the 17th they were arrested again, this time for contempt of the court's injunction. It had become apparent that the strike was disintegrating, that public opinion was against it, that it was doomed to failure. The Union had already made an unsuccessful effort to open negotiations for a return to work on favorable terms. So, when the leaders were arrested this second time, they declined to give bail and elected to go to prison while the strike petered out, and to litigate the validity of the injunction by *habeas corpus* proceedings.

The Federal troops were withdrawn from Chicago on the 20th.

Of course, there were voices to cry out that disorders increased during the few days which followed the army's entry into Chicago, to argue that the troops were not needed, and that their presence did more harm than good. Governor Altgeld, of Illinois, protested that the President had no power to send them to the city. But when the military are called out to prevent trouble there are always some people who persuade themselves that any subsequent disturbances have

been occasioned by the precautions. No impressive evidence has ever been offered to prove that the regulars caused violence in 1894. On the contrary, it seems certain that their arrival in Chicago put a check upon the disorders which had begun, and that their use in that city had a distinct moral effect in other places as well. Altgeld overlooked the fact that, from the Administration's point of view (and from the general public's), Illinois was merely one scene of disturbances which extended throughout the West, Mid-West, and Southwest; that the Government had to select a strategic point for a show of firmness, and that its choice could not be made to wait upon the diverse preferences which local authorities might entertain about local situations. He seems also to have evolved an indefensible theory that, since the Constitution expressly authorizes a Governor to call on the President for troops, it compels the President, by implication, to wait for such a requisition before employing them.

In using the army to suppress disorder in 1894, Cleveland and Olney may be said to have confirmed a correct construction of the Federal Government's powers, rather than to have enlarged them. But undoubtedly they surprised the country, and made the deeper impression on it accordingly. They acted before the popular mind saw what was coming, and without waiting for anything like a popular mandate. Then, too, their action jostled rudely against a supposition which was still commonly made in 1894. Among the convictions which the Civil War had embedded in the country's political consciousness, and which nothing had yet shaken, was the idea that the Democratic Party must champion the States against the power of the Federal Government on every occasion. Yet here were Cleveland

and Olney not only throwing Federal troops into Illinois unbidden by her authorities, but keeping them there in spite of her Governor's protest and regardless of the fact that Illinois had contributed largely to the Democratic victory in 1892. As if to emphasize this abandonment of tradition, they relied upon a statute, among others, which had been passed in Grant's Administration as a measure of reconstruction. (R.S., sect. 5299.) What was more, they went ahead and discharged their duty to the country in that wise without vouchsafing so much as a word of regret or explanation for the Democrats, departed or still living, who had declaimed, fought, and protested about "States' rights" for two generations. Their action announced the end of a political era more convincingly than the most eloquent proclamation could have signalized it — announced that the theory of States' rights as Altgeld invoked it was now a discarded shibboleth, and that (with respect to anything like an Altgeldian political philosophy, at any rate) the Democratic Party was escaping from bondage to its memories of the Civil War. No language could have been more Federal in spirit than Olney's: "the soil of Illinois is the soil of the United States, and for all United States purposes the United States is there . . . not by license or comity, but as of right." One sentence which he issued to the press must have struck former secession Democrats as a truly brutal sentence for a Democratic Attorney-General to utter: "The notion that territory of any State is too sacred to permit the exercise thereon by the United States Government of any of its legitimate functions never had any legal existence, and, as a rule of conduct, became practically extinct with the close of the Civil War." Had words been needed when actions were so clear, none could

have breathed the Administration's faith in the country's integrity more reassuringly than those in which Cleveland was said to have exclaimed, "If it takes every dollar in the Treasury and every soldier in the United States Army to deliver a postal card in Chicago, that postal card shall be delivered."

Apart from the fact that the Administration's conduct set an example of the very highest value, there resulted from the action taken at Chicago one new judicial precedent of which the importance cannot be measured even now, and of which the latter-day implications are too complex for treatment here. The equity powers of the courts had never been invoked in this way. The end of the Chicago strike popularized a new weapon for use in industrial disputes, and Judge Woods's injunction was bitterly criticized by the labor organizations.

The reader will remember that Debs, committed to jail for contempt of the injunction, brought *habeas corpus* proceedings to test its validity. Of the progress and outcome of those proceedings an account can be given in Olney's own words. The case went against Debs in the Circuit Court, was appealed, and was argued in the Supreme Court on March 26th and 27th, 1895.

"The Chicago equity bills" (says the Memorandum) "had rested the Government's case on two grounds, first, on its general equity powers to interfere by injunction in a perfectly clear case of threatened irreparable injury, and, second, upon the provisions of the Sherman Anti-Trust Law of 1890. While not abandoning this second ground of jurisdiction, I made no argument about it and left the brief and the oral discussion of that part of the case to my assistant, Mr. Whitney. I argued the case solely upon the first point — telling the Court at the outset that I desired the case decided, if possible, with reference to it and not by reason of an experimental piece of legislation like the Act of 1890. As is shown by the report of the case, the Court took my view, eliminating the Act of 1890 from consideration, and, what seldom happens when a new and grave constitutional question arises, unanimously deciding for the Government on the grounds stated by Mr. Justice Brewer in delivering the opinion. The case for Debs was ably and passionately presented by Judge (Lyman) Trumbull and Messrs. (S. S.) Gregory and (Clarence S.) Darrow, of the Chicago Bar. Their efforts surprised me, however, and I think the Court also, by their rather obvious avoidance of the crucial legal problem involved and their resort to heated declamations about individual liberty, the right to trial by jury, etc., etc. It was not possible, however, to doubt the sincerity of at least two of Debs's counsel. Judge Trumbull, an Illinois United States Senator during the Civil War, for many years an eminent Republican leader and statesman and the author (?) of 'The Fourteenth Amendment to the United States Constitution,' was in the eighties in 1895, and while he spoke with great feeling, argued from sentimental rather than legal premises. His colleague, Mr. Darrow, did the same, although a young man, somewhere between thirty and forty, who had been counsel for one of the leading railroads centering in Chicago — I think the Illinois Central — and who had thrown up his job because of his interest in the wage-earner and his desire to side with him rather than with the capitalist on the various issues arising between them and daily becoming graver and more difficult of settlement. From a strictly legal point of view the best argument was made by Mr. (S. S.) Gregory, who had been city solicitor of Chicago, and who, as I understood, unlike his associates, who acted gratuitously and from sympathy, was professionally retained and paid.

"The evening of the day when the cases were argued, I gave a large dinner to which I invited the Debs counsel, Mrs. Trumbull, and any other ladies who had come with them to Washington. They accepted and were quite surprised as well as pleased at the attention, as they had apparently got the notion that, as the representatives of Debs, they would not be considered within the pale of respectable Washington society."

Gustavus Myers: THE SUPREME COURT DECISION AS EVIDENCE OF CLASS BIAS

SEVEN days after its obliterating the income-tax law, the Supreme Court of the United States handed down a decision which was then regarded, and has been since, by both legal profession and lay public, as one of the most extraordinary on record. . . .

This decision was in the Debs case, which was a result of the great strike of the railway workers in 1894. That strike originated in the grievances of the workers in the Pullman Company's shops. . . .

The company refusing to consider their grievances, the workers, on May 11, 1894,

Excerpted from Gustavus Myers, *History of the Supreme Court of the United States* (Chicago: Charles H. Kerr & Company, 1912), pp. 618–625. Used with permission.

declared a strike. The interests of the Pullman Company and nearly all of the large railroad systems were closely associated; the same magnates were often found as stockholders in both; and by reason of its immense profits, the company was continually extending its holdings in railroad lines. At present the only three railroads in which the Pullman Company has no interest are the St. Paul, the New York, New Haven and Hartford, and the Great Northern.

It was, therefore, with a view to compelling the Pullman Company to come to terms that the American Railway Union, under the leadership of Eugene V. Debs, declared a general sympathetic strike. But there were other strong reasons. For twelve years the General Managers' Association, representing twenty-four railroads centering or terminating in Chicago, had been in aggressive existence. Leagued together in this powerful organization, these representatives of the railroad magnates were reducing the wages of railroad workers below the level of subsistence, and on the other hand were combined for the purpose of extorting high passenger and freight rates. In law it was a conspiracy in restraint of trade, but it is needless to say that no writ of arrest had ever been issued against a single member of the General Managers' Association. Neither did any court presume to issue an injunction, sweeping or qualified. Railroad workers, agitating for better conditions, were discharged and blacklisted, yet for this offense the General Managers' Association was not even questioned by the authorities. This systematic campaign against the railroad workers led to the formation of the American Railway Union, composed of employes, and was one of the contributing causes of the great strike of 1894.

Repeating their successful ruse used at Pittsburg in the strike of 1877, the railroad corporations caused cheap, worn-out freight cars to be set on fire, and then forthwith accused the strikers of violence and rioting. This charge proclaimed through twenty thousand subservient newspapers, prejudiced the general public mind, and was immediately seized upon as a pretext for the ordering out of Federal troops. Evidently Governor Altgeld knew the real facts, for he refused to call upon the President for troops. In violation of the law, and against Altgeld's protest, President Cleveland, ostensibly to quell rioting, but in reality to interfere with strikers assembling and picketing, hurried Federal soldiers to Illinois. At the same time Federal judges, some of whom had been attorneys for the railroads involved, issued unprecedented injunctions which even went so far as to forbid the strikers from persuading fellow workers to quit work.

One of these injunctions was issued by the Federal judge, Peter S. Grosscup, at Chicago. It was notorious that Grosscup owed his position to the influence of corporations; recent disclosures regarding his conduct both before he was a judge and since that time are supposed to have been instrumental in causing his recent resignation. Grosscup's brother, Benjamin, was a Northern Pacific Railroad attorney. On July 3, 1908, Charles H. Aldrich, a Chicago attorney who had originally indorsed Grosscup for the judgeship, sent to United States Attorney-General Bonaparte a communication in which he accused Grosscup of having asked railroads for free transportation for himself and family and for others. . . .

It was Grosscup who, at a critical stage in the strike, caused Debs and his associates to be haled up for contempt of court, and it was Grosscup who, acting as prosecutor, judge and jury all in one, convicted them of contempt of court, and sentenced them to jail.

Debs, on January 14, 1895, applied to the Supreme Court for a writ of habeas corpus.

His counsel, Lyman Trumbull, a noted lawyer who himself had represented corporations, began his argument by reciting the circumstances of "the extraordinary proceeding under which the prisoners were deprived of liberty." This action was begun by the filing of a bill of equity in the name of the United States under the direction of Attorney-General Olney. As we have seen, Olney had been a railroad director. The bill was unsigned by anyone, and "has attached to it an affidavit of George I. Allen, an unknown person, having, so far as the record shows, no connection with the case, stating that he has read the bill and 'believes the statements contained therein are true.'" Was there anything unlawful, Trumbull asked, in the American Railway Union calling upon its members to quit work? If not, then Debs and associates were not engaged in any unlawful combination or conspiracy. The boycott of the Pullman cars was, as the bill clearly showed, not to obstruct commerce, but for an entirely different purpose. Refusing to work, Trumbull went on, was no crime. Although such an action might incidentally delay the mails or interfere with interstate commerce, it was a lawful act and no offense. The act of Congress to protect trade and commerce against unlawful restraints and monopoly did not apply to the case stated in the bill; if so, Trumbull said, it was unconstitutional.

Justice Brewer delivered the decision of an unanimous Court. The remarkable sight was now presented of this "great and honorable court" deciding the case upon a point in no way involved, thus violating one of the most fundamental principles of law. Brewer denied Debs' petition upon the ground that he and associates had obstructed interstate commerce traffic by derailing and wrecking engines and trains, and assaulting and disabling railroad employes. If this were true, why was it that no such criminal action had ever been brought against Debs? And if it were true, Debs could have been convicted and sentenced to prison for a long term, instead of getting the sentence of six months in jail for contempt of court that the Supreme Court of the United States on May 27, 1895, thus affirmed. In the very act of sending Debs to jail the Supreme Court established (as an entering wedge) the ominous precedent and principle that the Federal anti-trust law applied to combinations of wage workers.

Of the Justices sanctioning this decision, these particulars, repeated here, are pertinent as indicating class bias:

Chief Justice Fuller had been counsel for Marshall Field, chief owner of the Pullman works, and he had represented the Chicago, Burlington and Quincy Railroad and other railroad capitalists and interests.

Justice Field had been placed on the Supreme Court Bench by the Central Pacific and the Southern Pacific Railroad interests.

Field's nephew, Brewer, was sponsored by the same and allied interests.

Justice Gray was a capitalist with varied interests and connections.

Justice Shiras had represented the Baltimore and Ohio Railroad system.

Justice Brown had represented the Vanderbilt and other railroads as counsel in Michigan, and was a corporation stockholder.

Justice White was a rich Louisiana sugar planter. . . .

Charles Warren: THE SUPREME COURT DECISION

THE year 1895 was notable for the decision of three great cases in which the public took the liveliest interest. In the first, decided January 21, the Court passed for the first time on the application of the Sherman Anti-Trust Act to commercial corporations, and in *United States v. E. C. Knight Co.*, 156 U. S. 1, — the *Sugar Trust Case*, — held that, on the facts presented, the corporations involved in the combination refining sugar were not engaged in interstate commerce. The result was a disappointment to those who relied on the Act as a destroyer of the trusts. The second case involved the constitutionality of the Income Tax. . . .

Equally violent assaults upon the Court followed from a decision rendered, seven days later, in the third great case, *In re Debs*, 158 U. S. 564. For the past five years, legal questions growing out of labor strikes had been presented more and frequently to the inferior Federal Courts through applications for injunctions, chiefly by owners and Federal receivers of railroads. In 1893, the Supreme Court had for the first time been called upon to deal with the subject. . . . The *Debs Case* grew out of the great Pullman strike and riots of 1894, and its decision, on May 25, 1895, is to be regarded as one of the datum posts in American legal history. The Court, in a notable opinion by Judge Brewer, upheld an injunction issued by the lower Court, restraining the defendant from obstructing trains engaged in interstate commerce or in carrying the mails. . . .

This decision, sustaining President Cleveland's energetic action in employing both the military and civil forces of the Government to end the strike, caused a great sensation, and was widely indorsed by conservative and patriotic men, as a strong support to the stability of the Nation. Such an application of National power to a labor situation, however, was a long step towards centralization of authority; and as a legal writer said, while "all must applaud the promptness and vigor with which the Federal power acted, saving the country perhaps from a reign of anarchy and bloodshed . . . slowly but inevitably one after another of these State police powers is being brought within the limits of Federal jurisdiction." The decision gave great offense to certain labor elements in the community; and as it was rendered only a week after the decision in the *Income Tax Case*, it was criticized as an illustration of the prejudice of the Court in favor of capital.

The public discussion and hostility which grew out of these three decisions in 1895, each of which was asserted to have been in favor of "the propertied class," was signalized by the insertion of a plank in the platform adopted at the National Convention of the Democratic Party in Chicago in 1896, which, in that campaign of somewhat hysterical political passion, was termed an anarchical attack on the Judiciary. [. . . The controverted plank was as follows: " . . . We denounce arbitrary interference by Federal authorities in local affairs as a violation of the Constitution of the United States and as a crime against free institutions, and we especially object to government by injunction as a new and highly dangerous form of oppression by which Federal

Excerpted from Charles Warren, *The Supreme Court in United States History* (Boston: Little, Brown and Company, 1923), pp. 421–428. Reprinted by permission of Little, Brown and Company Copyright 1922, 1926 by Little, Brown and Company; 1950, 1954 by Charles Warren.

Judges, in contempt of the law of the States and rights of citizens, become at once Legislators, Judges and executioners; and we approve the bill, passed at the last session of the United States Senate and now pending in the House, relative to contempts in Federal Courts, providing for trials by jury in certain cases of contempt."] In reality, the plank was an extremely mild expression of views, when compared with many former criticisms which had been made in conservative newspapers and law journals. The general situation, however, and especially the Income Tax decision, produced a reawakening of the type of assault on the Court which had appeared successively in 1821, 1833, 1857, 1868, 1885 — namely the demand that the Court should be shorn of its alleged "usurped" power to pass upon the validity of Acts of Congress. All the fallacious arguments which had been used in previous eras were reproduced, and, as formerly, reiterated without any attempt to ascertain the historical facts as to the "usurpation.". . . Most violent and voluble of all the Court's critics was Governor Sylvester Pennoyer of Oregon, who wrote: ". . . The Supreme Court has not contented itself

with its undisputed judicial prerogative of interpreting the laws of Congress which may be ambiguous, but it has usurped the legislative prerogative of declaring what the laws shall not be. Our constitutional government has been supplanted by a judicial oligarchy. . . ."

Coincident with these attacks on the Supreme Court, there had arisen severe criticisms of the extension of the power of the National Judiciary through its increasingly wide exercise of equity jurisdiction and extensive employment of injunctions. "Government by injunction" had become a term of judicial opprobrium constantly echoed by the laboring class. . . .

In 1896, the Court announced the broadest definition of the right of Congress to legislate for the general welfare when it sustained the taking by eminent domain of the Gettysburg battlefield for a National cemetery. . . . This decision, taken in connection with the *Debs Case,* showed that the Court was practically prepared to support any action taken by the National Government and reasonably necessary for its self-preservation and welfare.

Willard L. King: THE DEBS CASE

THERE are many versions of the Debs case: the communist version, the labor leader's version, the social worker's version, the industrialist's version, and finally, the lawyer's version, which is what I am to tell you about today.

I have read the records and the opinions of the courts in the case and also the voluminous briefs and arguments of counsel. I have secured some light from the old letter books of Mr. Stephen

Strong Gregory who was Debs's attorney in the case. Finally, by a stroke of luck, I have found what I believe to be the only copy in existence of a complete typewritten transcript of the evidence. It fills four large folio volumes.

The Newberry Library in Chicago has made available to me eight large scrap books, compiled by the Pullman Company at the time, of newspaper clippings about the strike. But unfortunately, on

Lecture at Amherst College, November 19, 1952.

this subject historians have relied too much upon newspapers — always a dubious source where court proceedings are involved.

The Pullman strike was not legally pertinent to the Debs case and the court rigorously excluded testimony concerning it. I claim no special knowledge regarding it. I have always assumed — perhaps wrongfully — that in that strike, like most strikes, something could be said on both sides. As I understand it, following the hard times of 1893 the railroads had stopped buying Pullman cars. The Company was struggling to hold its organization together instead of closing down tight. It had built a lot of cars that it could not sell. But apparently its management failed to bring home this plight to its workers. Such a failure of communication would be unforgivable under modern standards of industrial relations.

The Pullman Company made other errors that industry has since learned to avoid. It had built a beautiful, modern brick town so that its workers would not live in slums. But that meant regimentation. And the strikers complained more about abusive and tyrannical foremen and paternalism than they did about the 20% wage cut. Industry has since learned that workers value independence and self-respect as much as they do adequate wages.

However, the criticism of the Pullman Company made in some recent American histories to the effect that it then had a large surplus from its prosperous years from which it could have paid wages to workers, whose product it could not sell, is hardly justifiable. The directors of a corporation cannot lawfully give away its surplus to its workers or to any one else. They would be condemned by the courts, removed, and held personally liable if they did any such thing.

The story of the Debs case must start with Debs, himself. Eugene V. Debs, born in 1855 of Alsatian parents in Terre Haute, Indiana, had a limited schooling, but educated himself to a remarkable degree. In his teens, he became a railroad fireman but soon quit railroading at his mother's behest. She feared that, like many boys she had known, he would be injured or killed. So Debs got a job as a clerk with a wholesale grocer. Shortly thereafter the union of railroad firemen was formed and Debs became an officer of it. He was a marked man, 6 feet 5 inches tall, and his face radiated intelligence and friendship. Well read and facile in speech, he became very popular in the Union. Lincoln Steffens, his fellow Socialist, later said of him: "He was the kindliest and the foolishest man I have ever known." Debs became editor of the national magazine of the Firemen's Union and the moving spirit in its organization.

Then, as now, railroad unions were organized in separate brotherhoods. Debs thought there should be one union of all railroad workers. In 1893 he left the Firemen's Union to organize the American Railway Union. Early in its organization this Union had a great victory in resisting a wage cut made by James J. Hill on the Great Northern Railroad. Debs's Union struck and he succeeded in gaining the support of business men in St. Paul and securing an arbitration that reduced the wage cut.

This success gave further impetus to the organization of the American Railway Union. By June of 1894, he claimed 125,000 to 150,000 members. Among Debs's members were about 2,000 employees of the Pullman Company at its car plant in Pullman, Illinois, constituting about half of the employees of the Company there. Debs was deeply moved by their complaints but strongly advised them not to strike. However, when the Company refused to arbitrate their protests at a further wage cut, a portion of them did strike and the Company immediately closed down its plant.

A few weeks later, the first annual convention of the American Railway Union met in Chicago. At the convention, the Pullman workers appeared and insisted that their Union do something for them. Debs exhausted every effort to aid them without taking drastic action. It was the worst possible time for a strike. With 100,000 men out of work in Chicago, the places of strikers could be easily filled. Debs successively appointed three committees to see the Pullman management and try to secure an arbitration. But the Pullman Company responded that they had nothing to arbitrate — their plant was indefinitely closed. The Union then voted $2,000 in relief funds for the Pullman strikers, which was about the amount they had paid in dues. However the Pullman workers insisted that something more effective be done. Debs then recommended that the members of the American Railway Union boycott and refuse to handle any Pullman cars until the Pullman Company would arbitrate its strike. Soberer heads in the Union resisted this plea; the Union was not well enough organized, they argued, to carry through such a boycott. But Debs's eloquence prevailed and the convention ordered that its members boycott all Pullman cars. However, no strike of any kind was authorized by the convention. This boycott was clearly unlawful. By this time, it had become established that a peaceful strike for higher wages or to redress grievances was perfectly lawful. A man had a legal right to quit his work at any time and he could also legally quit in unison with his fellow employees. But the courts in a long line of decisions, both

in England and America, had condemned a boycott such as this. It was a malicious, unlawful conspiracy to force the employer to injure someone else.

Debs's scheme was even more unlawful. The railroads were of course bound by contract to carry the Pullman cars. No matter how peaceful a strike might have been, it was certainly illegal to advise employees to disobey their employers' lawful orders. Without any grievance against the railroads, the members of the American Railway Union started to cut off the Pullman cars. Sometimes they were left on a sidetrack; sometimes they were derailed. Indeed Debs's telegrams to his members at the beginning of the strike read: "Boycott against Pullman Company is in full force and effect and no Pullman cars are to be handled and hauled. Convention ordered boycott of Pullman cars and this means they will be cut out and de-tracked." Not sidetracked, you will note, but de-tracked. But whether the cars were sidetracked or de-tracked this boycott was more unlawful than the sitdown strike. It was illegal then — it would be equally unlawful now. Trainmen cutting off Pullman cars were of course immediately discharged and what might now be called "wildcat strikes" followed on most of the railroads in the West.

At once great violence erupted. In general, the engineers, conductors and trainmen did not strike. Firemen, to a limited extent, and switchmen, to a somewhat larger extent, did strike. But only a minor fraction of the railroad workers left their jobs. Thus on the Rock Island Railroad with 12,000 employees, there were only 522 strikers, — but they stopped all traffic on the road for five days. On most of the railroads, however, traffic was delayed but not completely interrupted. The strikers piled rails on the tracks, ditched trains, cut the air brakes on the trains, burned the railroads' property, turned over cars on the tracks and beat and injured the men who were still working.

Grover Cleveland, a man of immense courage and determination, was then President of the United States. His Attorney General, Richard Olney of Boston, a graduate of Brown and Harvard Law Schools, later became Secretary of State, and holds a high place among American Attorneys General. Some historians have made the point that, in his private practice, he had represented certain railroads and had at one time been a Director of the C. B. & Q. Railroad. But it would have been rather difficult in 1893 for a President to have found a competent Attorney General who had not at some stage of his practice represented a railroad.

The criticism has been made of Attorney General Olney that he tried from the first to break the strike. We all believe that Government should maintain a neutral attitude toward a strike unless there is violence or insufferable invasion of the public interest. Government should be an umpire; not a strike-breaker. Olney was certainly not neutral. But this boycott was no strike at all in the sense that we now understand a strike. No negotiations were had with the railroads; in fact, no communications were made to them; the boycott started with violence and the strikers tried by force and sabotage to stop all railroad traffic. The railroads could end the boycott only by violating their contracts with the Pullman Company, thus incurring colossal damages.

The problem was first presented to the President by the Post Office Department which complained that its mails were being obstructed in Chicago and on the west coast. Olney immediately directed the United States District Attorneys to arrest those who obstructed the mails. Apparently as soon as the riots in Chicago occurred, Olney suggested to President Cleveland the use of United States troops to quell them. Cleveland responded that, without a request from the Governor of the State, he was unwilling to use the Federal troops for this purpose, unless the process of the United States courts was obstructed.

Olney conceived the theory that the United States could secure an injunction against the forcible interference with the mails and inter-state commerce. The labor injunction was not new at that time. Several such injunctions had previously been issued at the behest of an employer to protect his property and to enjoin violence against his workers. But no such injunction had previously been secured by the United States. It was a settled rule of law that no injunction could be issued against crimes as such. A person accused of crime had a constitutional right to trial by jury. But a man charged with violation of an injunction did not get a jury trial; his trial was before the court for contempt. However, many violations of injunctions were also crimes. So the fact that a violation of an injunction would be a crime was no basis for denying the injunction if property rights were being violated. Chief Justice Marshall had held that the United States had property rights in the mail. True, the bulk of the letters did not belong to it but the mail sacks did and a substantial part of the mail, Marshall had pointed out, was the property of the Government consisting of letters passing from one Federal officer to another.

Furthermore, the Constitution vested in Congress complete power over commerce "among the several states and with the Indian tribes." Congress had exercised this power by declaring that all railroads constituted highways for inter-state commerce. Congress had passed the Inter-State Commerce Act completely regulating the railroads engaged in inter-state commerce. Several precedents existed for an injunction by the United States to enjoin obstruction of waterways which had also been declared to be highways for inter-state commerce.

In addition, Congress had recently passed the Sherman Act, which, though designed to operate against trusts and monopolies, by its express terms authorized an injunction against a conspiracy to obstruct inter-state commerce. Olney's theory therefore was that an injunction proceeding could be brought to enjoin Debs and his associates from forcible interference with the mails and with inter-state commerce. Olney employed Edwin Walker, an able lawyer of Chicago, as Special United States District Attorney to secure such an injunction. Complaint has since been made that he should not have employed an attorney connected with one of the railroads. Like the Attorney General, Mr. Walker was a leading lawyer in general practice who had sometimes been employed by the St. Paul Railroad. In 1893, the year before, he had been General Counsel of the World's Columbian Exposition. The criticism of the Attorney General for his selection of Mr. Walker does not seem to me justifiable. But any other competent lawyer would doubtless have won the case as he did.

Walker prepared a bill for injunction in accordance with the Attorney General's instructions and filed it in the United States Circuit Court in Chicago on July 2, 1894. The rioting was then rampant and an injunction was at once issued by Judges Grosscup and Woods.

Through the years much criticism has been made of the broad scope of this injunction. It enjoined Debs and all of the officers of the American Railway Union from obstructing or interfering with the operation of the railroads. It did not enjoin a strike. It did not enjoin any individual from quitting work in unison with his fellow employees or otherwise. Particularly complaint has been made that Debs was enjoined from peaceful persuasion of the employees to strike. But the injunction did not prohibit that. It very properly prohibited Debs from persuading the employees of the railroads not to perform their duties, that is from cutting off Pullman cars. Of course the main purport of the injunction was against violence and the destruction of property.

Another complaint that has been made is that the injunction was issued without notice to the defendants. The Federal statutes at that time required notice before an injunction could be issued unless the circumstances were such that peril would occur if notice were given. In that event a court could issue a temporary injunction and a prompt hearing could be set on whether it should be made permanent. Since riots were then going on, cars were being burned and derailed, and employees of the railroad were being beaten and injured, it is not surprising that the court in its discretion issued the injunction without notice. In any event the defendants had the right immediately to come into court and have the injunction vacated if it had been improperly issued. And if the injunction were too broad in its scope, they had the right immediately to move to strike out its excessive mandates. Although Debs was surrounded by the ablest attorneys, he made no such motions at any time.

Some American historians have suggested that Judges Grosscup and Woods were partisan or even venal and corrupt in issuing this injunction. No basis exists for this charge as anyone may see by reading the biographies of these Judges in the Dictionary of American Biography. I have found some letters in Mr. Gregory's letter book bearing on this subject.

Thus Gregory, Debs's attorney, wrote his client on the day before the Supreme Court released Debs on bail:

"I see from time to time various abusive expressions and statements as to the Court of the U. S. attributed to you. I presume they are frequently exaggerated and distorted — but venture to suggest moderation in such public expression as you may make upon the subject of your prosecution and the action generally of the Federal Courts. This is by no means inconsistent with a firm, resolute and dignified attitude on the part of yourselves and associates. Such will in my judgment be more impressive and worthy of men of determination and earnestness than what might seem to be vituperative and hysterical abuse of those who, having grave responsibilities and solemn duties in this regard, must meet them according to their best intelligence and their own standards of conscience and public duty."

The next month Mr. Gregory again cautioned Debs, now out on bail, on the subject of his vituperation against the Courts:

"At the risk of seeming to be unreasonable I venture to write you a line to caution you as to your address Thursday evening. There is great eloquence and power in moderate statement. I do not think we can prove that the railroad companies burned up their own cars, nor do I by any means feel sure that they will not bring on this case for trial again, and I think your statements on both of those

points ought to be made with some reserve and with due regard to actual conditions. Further than that I would expressly avoid anything but the most impersonal discussion of the action of the courts, and that without bitterness or anything approaching vituperation."

A few years after the Debs case, Judge Grosscup was promoted by President McKinley to the Circuit Court of Appeals. In this connection, Mr. Gregory, a Democrat, wrote to Judge Grosscup: "I can not think there is anything worthy of notice in rumors of opposition to yr nomination in the Senate on account of yr course in the Debs case. However if you deem the matter worthy of attention, I, and [I] have no doubt Mr. Darrow, would be willing to write to any Senators or take any other action that might be deemed expedient to aid speedy confirmation. . . . I may perhaps here say what I never have said to you [:] that I have often, in private conversation, instanced the Debs case in yr court as one in which the scales of Justice were held with even hand where with a weaker man they would have been strongly inclined against the defendants' interests."

These letters from Debs's counsel in the case ought to end the repetition by reputable historians of Debs's charges of partisanship, venality and corruption against the Courts who heard his case. It has been said that history repeats itself but historians repeat each other. Much of the history written in America during the past twenty-five years has been unconsciously colored by the Communist hullabaloo.

The injunction was issued on July 2nd and was at once served on Debs and the officers of the Union. Debs himself was not served until 8:00 A. M. on the morning of July 4th. As soon as the injunction was issued, however, it was published in the newspapers and posted on the railroad premises and at the scenes of the riots. At such a riot where a mail train had been ditched, the United States marshal, standing at the door of a mail car, read the injunction to the crowd of strikers and ordered them to disperse. He was cursed and jeered, and some of the rioters exclaimed: "To hell with the United States court." The mob then derailed other cars to block the tracks.

Attorney General Olney had suggested to the United States District Attorney in Chicago that if the riots did not stop with the injunction and he deemed United States troops to be necessary, he should sign a letter to that effect and secure letters from the United States Judges to the same purport. After the marshal's experience with the mob, a telegram was sent to the Attorney General signed by the United States Marshal and District Attorney and the United States Circuit Judge to the effect that the rioting continued, unabated, and that troops were needed to quell it. Mr. Olney presented this message to President Cleveland, who called a cabinet meeting to consider it. As a result, 5,000 United States troops from Fort Sheridan moved into the city.

This action, without a request by the Governor of the State, provoked a sharp complaint by Governor Altgeld of Illinois. President Cleveland in response insisted that the United States had the right to use the Army to overcome obstructions to the mails and inter-state commerce. Cleveland, who was a man of immense force, said privately that if it required the entire United States Army to deliver a postal card to Chicago, that card would be delivered. When Governor Altgeld continued his complaints, the President cut him off with the comment that it would be better for all concerned to devote themselves to quelling the riots rather than discussing the jurisdiction.

Some American historians have condemned President Cleveland for moving in the troops so quickly, intimating that he was over-persuaded by Attorney General Olney. It has been suggested that it would have been safe to have delayed the arrival of the troops for two more days and the situation *might* have been handled without them. Historians have noted that an examination of the newspapers disclosed that there was no violence on the 4th and 5th of July immediately following the entry of the troops. However, the evidence in the contempt case shows that the troops arrived on the evening of July 3rd and that there were many mobs that stopped trains and assaulted crews on the 4th and 5th of July. It is not surprising that the Courts eventually held that the President's action was fully justified. The violence and rioting continued unabated on the 6th and the 7th and was finally brought under control only by the state militia and the Federal troops.

Mr. Samuel Gompers, the president of the American Federation of Labor, then came to Chicago and, with his officers and the officers of the Railroad Brotherhoods, conferred with Debs and the officers of the American Railway Union. Debs was urging a general country-wide strike of all union men in support of his boycott. However, Mr. Gompers and the other union men pointed out to him that success in his boycott was impossible in the light of overwhelming public opinion against it and told Debs that he should secure the best settlement available. Debs then addressed his first communication to the railroads. Written in his flamboyant style, it sought sympathy for his members and offered, in view of the violence that had occurred, to terminate the boycott if the railroads would take back the strikers. The railroads refused to receive this communication and the strikes ended.

Debs subsequently testified before the United States Strike Commission that the strike was broken, not by the Army, but by the United States Courts, in restraining the officers of the Union, as he put it, "from discharging their duties." This statement has been repeated by many historians. It is hardly accurate. First: The injunction was against violence — not a peaceful strike. Second: The injunction did not end the violence. The troops did that. And Third: Debs was not arrested for violation of the injunction until July 17th after the strike had completely failed.

Debs and his officers, when arrested for contempt, were immediately released on bond. Under pretext of serving some papers, the United States Marshal seized the files in the office of the Union. This seizure was entirely wrong. As soon as Attorney General Olney heard of it, he telegraphed that the papers should be returned to the Union. Mr. Walker, his counsel in Chicago, took this telegram as a personal criticism and remonstrated. Later, however, Walker recognized that he had been wrong in condoning the seizure and wrote Mr. Olney that the nervous strain that Walker had been under accounted for his attitude. As soon as Judge Grosscup heard of the seizure, he, too, instantly ordered the papers returned. Mr. Debs later said that Judge Grosscup in effect apologized to him in open court for the seizure of the papers.

Debs and his officers then went on trial before Judge Woods for contempt. This trial lasted several weeks and resulted in this voluminous record. The United States offered 77 witnesses of the riots and the alleged instigation of the vio-

lence by Debs and the officers of the American Railway Union. The proof was overwhelming. The defendants offered no witnesses to refute it. Some of Debs's associates were called to the witness stand by the Government. They refused to testify, claiming their constitutional right against self-incrimination under the Fifth Amendment.

Debs's responsibility for the violence was also proved indubitably. True, in his telegrams to his subordinates urging them to tie up the railroads tight, he frequently used the words: "Commit no violence." But it was clear, as the court found, that these words were only to gain public sympathy. To Debs, violence meant assaulting and beating people. He was a kindly man and would not have intentionally hurt a fly. But to him, it was not violence to sidetrack or de-track the Pullman cars; it was not violence to spike switches and derail trains; to tip over cars and obstruct the tracks; to cut the air hose, to give false signals to moving trains; to pull the engineers and firemen from their cabs if by threats and abuse they could not be forced out of them; to smash and burn the railroad property. Over a thousand freight cars, many of them loaded with valuable freight, were burned by the mobs. The courts disagreed with Debs on his conception of violence. He had instructed that the strikers and their sympathizers wear a white ribbon in their lapels and the testimony showed conclusively that the rioters and particularly their leaders wore these ribbons. In fact, some of them wore a white badge with a picture of Debs on it. They issued orders in his name and he released by written orders certain cars and trains held by the mobs. Others he refused to release.

The Government forced the telegraph companies to produce Debs's telegrams during the strike. In their sworn answer in the contempt proceeding, Debs and his associates denied categorically that these telegrams were sent or caused to be sent by them or authorized or approved by them. However, it was proved that the telegrams were not only signed in Debs's name but were sent at half rate on his personal frank, and were afterwards paid for by the American Railway Union. Besides, many of them were in answer to telegrams received by Debs. Debs's telegrams contained many expressions such as "If your Company refuses to boycott Pullman, tie it up." "Knock it to them as hard as possible." "Pay no attention to injunction orders."

Under the evidence there could only be one result of this trial: the defendants were found guilty of violating the injunction. Debs was given six months in jail and his subordinate officers three months each.

The position of Debs's attorneys in the trial court was difficult. It is reminiscent of the story often told at the Bar of the young lawyer who consulted his old partner about a criminal case that the young man was defending. His client, with the stolen silver in a sack, had run into the arms of a policeman a block from a house that had been burglarized. There did not seem to be much defense. The old lawyer after hearing the story, said: "Your only defense is the conspiracy."

"What conspiracy?" said the youngster.

"Why the horrid conspiracy of the man whose house was burglarized with the police and State's Attorney to railroad your poor client to the penitentiary."

The conspiracy defense adopted by Debs's counsel was the conspiracy of the railroads with the Attorney General to railroad Debs to prison. The particular villain selected in this case was the General Managers' Association of the railroads. In every city like Chicago, the railroads have a clearing house. Such an association has existed in Chicago from 1886 to the present date. This harmless organization was accused of all the crimes in the calendar. It is surprising to find many American historians still repeating these fictitious charges. They didn't fool the Judge and they wouldn't fool any lawyer for a minute.

The attorneys for Debs now faced the question of appeal. It would clearly be fatal to bring before an upper court the murderous record of the trial in the contempt proceeding. The evidence was all on one side and it was overwhelming. Debs had employed some of the ablest lawyers in the United States. They evolved a plan of taking an appeal and omitting the record of the trial. Their plan was to apply for an original writ of *habeas corpus* in the Supreme Court on the ground that the whole injunction proceeding had been unlawful. By this device they could include in the record only the bill, the injunction, and the finding of contempt, omitting the evidence.

Let me tell you who Debs's counsel were.

First, there was Senator Lyman Trumbull. He had been Lincoln's early rival, both in law and in politics. Prior to 1855, Lincoln and Trumbull were the two outstanding lawyers in Illinois. Then they had been rival candidates for the United States Senate in 1855 and Lincoln had finally thrown his support to Trumbull to save the Free-state forces from defeat. Trumbull had thereafter been one of Lincoln's close friends. Trumbull was also a friend of Chief Justice Fuller and had taken an important part in securing Fuller's confirmation as Chief Justice in 1888. In Trumbull's later years in Chicago, it was his habit in teaching constitutional law at the Union College of Law when the class came to the 13th Amendment to say: "Gentlemen, this good right hand wrote this Amendment to the Constitution." Trumbull was Debs's lawyer in this case.

Another of Debs's lawyers was Stephen Strong Gregory, later President of the American Bar Association. Mr. Gregory fought every step of the way for Debs. At the time, Mr. Gregory's law partner was the son of Mr. Justice Harlan of the Supreme Court and the firm of Gregory & Harlan had succeeded to the practice of Chief Justice Fuller on his appointment as Chief Justice. Fuller, when in Chicago, used the offices of the firm as his headquarters.

Another of Debs's lawyers was a young man who resigned a position in the Law Department of the Northwestern Railroad to act for Debs. This lawyer afterwards became quite well known. His name was Clarence Darrow.

So you see Mr. Debs did not lack for adequate legal counsel.

As soon as Debs was lodged in jail in Woodstock, his attorneys sued out an original writ of *habeas corpus* in the Supreme Court of the United States. *Habeas corpus* is the ancient historic writ by which a person imprisoned without any legal warrant seeks his release. The original petition was presented to Justice John Marshall Harlan of the Supreme Court. He allowed Debs and his associates to be released on bail and referred the petition to the full Court for determination. Printed briefs and arguments were then filed by each counsel and the case was argued orally for two full days on March 25 and 26, 1895.

Since the case was before the Court on *habeas corpus,* the only question was whether the District Court in Chicago had jurisdiction to issue the original injunction. Debs's counsel took the position that the original injunction was a nullity so that it could be violated with impunity. They admitted that the facts stated in the original bill for injunction were true as alleged. They admitted that, if the court had power to issue the injunction, Debs had violated it. They were thus in no position to raise the points that the injunction had been too broad or that it had been wrongfully issued without notice.

They made three arguments: First, that there was no power in the Federal Government to secure an injunction against forcible interference with the mails because there was no Act of Congress specifically authorizing such an injunction. They argued that persons interfering with the passage of the mails should be indicted under existing statutes and should not be deprived of their constitutional right of trial by jury by being enjoined and prosecuted for contempt. A man should not be deprived of his constitutional right to trial by jury, they asserted, in the absence of a specific statute providing for such procedure. To this argument, the Government replied that the United States had property rights in the mails and the authorities were uniform to the effect that an injunction should be issued to protect property rights from unlawful interference.

Second, Debs's lawyers argued that there was no statute authorizing the Federal Government to secure an injunction against an interference with inter-state commerce. They attempted to distinguish the cases cited by the Attorney General where an injunction had been issued to enjoin the obstruction of a water highway of inter-state commerce by showing that the injunction in those cases was really issued to protect Government property on the water highway. Furthermore, Debs's attorneys argued that a physical obstruction of a waterway was not comparable to the obstruction of a railroad by a mob. A mob, they said, could be dispersed by the officers of the law.

The Government had to admit that, except for the Sherman Act, there was no statute specifically authorizing an injunction against interference with inter-state commerce. But the Attorney General argued that the power of the Federal Government over such commerce had been vested in it by the Constitution. Congress by the passage of the Inter-State Commerce Act and other Acts had fully occupied the field of regulation of inter-state commerce on the railroads. It had been held that no State could interfere with such inter-state commerce. If the Government could forbid a State from interfering, it certainly should be able to prevent any individual from interfering.

Third, Debs's attorneys argued that when the Sherman Act specifically gave power to the Federal Courts to enjoin a conspiracy in restraint of trade or commerce among the states, such conspiracies were limited by the context to those which Congress had in mind when the Act was passed, i.e., conspiracies in the nature of monopolies and trusts. Furthermore, they argued that if the Sherman Act were applicable, it was unconstitutional as an attempt to enforce a criminal statute by injunction, thus depriving the defendant in a criminal case of his constitutional right of trial by jury. Judge Woods in the trial court had based the jurisdiction squarely on the Sherman Act. Confronted with a choice of three bases for jurisdiction, he had chosen the Sherman Act as the clearest. He had said

nothing about the jurisdiction based on property rights in the mails or the unlimited control of the Federal Government over inter-state commerce.

Attorney General Olney made an able oral argument before the Supreme Court. It was afterwards printed and Debs, who had been an autograph collector all his life, wrote the Attorney General asking for an autographed copy of it. After due reflection, Olney sent it to him. During the period of the argument Attorney General Olney, as well as Chief Justice Fuller, gave dinner parties for Trumbull, Gregory and Darrow, Debs's attorneys.

In his argument Olney said at once that, without indicating in any way that the lower court was wrong in basing the jurisdiction on the Sherman Act, he would suggest that such a case should not be based on a "novel" or "experimental" statute or on any technical property rights in the mails. It should be founded instead, he said, on the unlimited power of the Federal Government over inter-state commerce and the necessity of protecting that commerce from such an obstruction and seizure as had occurred in this case. The Court in a unanimous opinion delivered by Mr. Justice Brewer, held the original injunction valid on these grounds. The Court based the injunction on the forcible interference with inter-state commerce and the mails. It did not sanction, as sometimes asserted, an injunction against a peaceful strike. The Court said: "A most earnest and eloquent appeal was made to us in eulogy of the heroic spirit of those who threw up their employment . . . not in defense of their own rights but in sympathy for and to assist others whom they believed to be wronged. We yield to none in our admiration of any act of heroism or self-sacrifice but we may be permitted to add that it is a lesson which cannot be learned too soon or too thoroughly . . . that no wrong, real or fancied, carries with it legal warrant to invite as a means of redress the cooperation of a mob with its accompanying acts of violence."

The Court disclaimed all intention to base the injunction on the Sherman Act, preferring to rest it upon the broader ground that any forcible interference with inter-state commerce and the mails might be enjoined by the United States. It followed that the lower court had jurisdiction to issue the injunction and Debs's petition for *habeas corpus* was denied.

Just a word about the Court that unanimously decided the case. Its roster compares favorably with that of any other Supreme Court in our history. Its Chief Justice was Melville Weston Fuller. Justice Samuel F. Miller, President Lincoln's appointee to the Court, who sat under Chief Justices Taney, Chase, Waite and Fuller, stated that Fuller was the best presiding judge that he had ever known. In our own times, Mr. Justice Holmes, who sat under Fuller, White, Taft and Hughes, declared that Fuller was the best presiding officer that he had ever known. As I have told you, Fuller was very close to Gregory and Trumbull, two of Debs's counsel. On that Court, and concurring in the opinion, were Justice Stephen J. Field, one of the staunchest guardians of civil rights that the Court has ever had; and Justice John Marshall Harlan, the great dissenter, and the father of Mr. Gregory's partner. No one ever charged Harlan with lack of humanity or lack of sympathy for the laboring man. Other Justices concurring in the opinion were Justice Horace Gray of Boston, perhaps the most scholarly Justice that the Court has ever had; Justice Henry Billings Brown of Detroit, a Yale

graduate, of distinguished ability; Justice George Shiras, Jr., of Pennsylvania, an honor graduate of Yale, and an outstanding lawyer and judge; and Justice Edward Douglass White, who later became Chief Justice. Finally there was Justice David Josiah Brewer, who wrote the opinion in which all of his colleagues concurred. Brewer had also graduated with honors from Yale and had served for fourteen years on the Supreme Court of Kansas when he was appointed to the Supreme Court of the United States in 1890. A man of sharp independence of judgment, no one ever accused him of laxity in the protection of the civil rights of the individual.

But I hear some of you asking, "Why has there been so much criticism of that Court?" "Why is it usually spoken of as mired in the mud of conservatism?" I think I can answer those questions. In 1911, the Marxists — that is the Socialists and Communists — despaired of ever making any progress in the United States until they could overcome the great reverence that the people then had for the Supreme Court. The result was the all-out attack on the Court that appeared in Gustavus Myers's *History of the Supreme Court* published in that year. Myers in a preface declared that he intended to tear down the Court as the "bulwark of capitalism" in the "conflict of the classes." His attack, though written in a more or less erudite style, sounds very much like the *Daily Worker* and contains egregious errors in every chapter — almost on every page. It makes a vitriolic attack on the Court on the basis among other things of the Debs case. I am ashamed to tell you that many American historians and political scientists have followed Myers in this attack. Thus Professor E. S. Corwin of Princeton, who has written two books in an effort to tear down the prestige of the Supreme Court, attempts to belittle Justice Brewer, the author of this opinion, in this language: "Even as early as 1883, we find Brewer sounding the alarm against Communism . . . and ten years later he is in full cry against . . . the fiend, fool or fanatic who would support these 'assassins of liberty'."

Of course, Debs never professed to be a Communist. He was, you will recall, on several occasions the Socialist candidate for President. It is worthy of note, however, that in 1918 he was sent to jail for counselling young men to resist the draft. Was this counsel based on Socialist pacifism or on Communist sympathy? In April, 1917, the St. Louis convention of the Socialist party had denounced the war. This action was consistent with the historic pacifism of the party. But Debs then made no anti-war speeches and later in the year 1917 he indicated that he favored some modification of the party's policy. But in the fall of 1917 came the October revolution in Russia, and Lenin rose to power. It was not until late June, 1918, and only a few days before our intervention in Russia that Debs counselled resistance to the draft in the United States. His conviction for this act was affirmed by a unanimous decision of the Supreme Court delivered by Mr. Justice Holmes. From his prison Debs then issued a long manifesto in eulogy of the Soviet government.

At the time it was decided in 1895, the Debs case was not regarded as a landmark. The *Harvard Law Review,* which reported all current cases of more than temporary significance, did not even mention it. The *Central Law Journal,* which then had a wide circulation in the legal profession, noted that the decision was unanimous and that any competent lawyer could have predicted the result. I very much fear that if it had not been for the Marxist attack on the Supreme Court, the Debs case would never have found a place in any American history.

Almont Lindsey: IN THE TOILS OF THE LAW

NOTHING contributed so much to the defeat of the strike as did the action taken by the federal courts. Between the Department of Justice and the federal judiciary there seemed to be a sympathetic understanding, and almost every move initiated by the former received the hearty support of the latter. Without this co-operation Richard Olney could not have blanketed every strike-infested region throughout the nation with an omnibus injunction – a weapon which proved very demoralizing to labor. From strike headquarters in Chicago, where the strategy of the American Railway Union was conceived, orders were issued to local organizations scattered over a wide area. Only in this manner could a united front be maintained and all activities co-ordinated among scores of striking groups from Michigan to California. As a result of the injunction, however, the central offices as well as all terminal offices of the union were restrained from performing many of the functions vital to the prosecution of the strike. For no less an offense than urging workers to join the struggle, union leaders were cited for contempt and arrested. Nor was this all, since the government

Excerpted from: Almont Lindsey, *The Pullman Strike* (Chicago: University of Chicago Press, 1942), pp. 274–305; 359–361. Reprinted by permission of The University of Chicago Press. Copyright by The University of Chicago. All rights reserved. Published December, 1942.

quickly impaneled grand juries that indicted hundreds of strikers and their
leaders for conspiracy.

In the judgment of Eugene Debs, the
collapse of the strike was not achieved by
the soldiers or railroad brotherhoods but
by the federal courts, which paralyzed
the leadership of the railway union. He
explained:

Our men were in a position that never
would have been shaken under any circumstances if we had been permitted to remain
among them . . . but once we were taken
from the scene of action and restrained from
sending telegrams or issuing the orders necessary, or answering questions; when the
minions of the corporations would be put to
work at such a place, for instance, as Nickerson, Kansas, where they would go and say
to the men that the men at Newton had gone
back to work, and Nickerson would wire me
to ask if that were true; no answer would
come to the message because I was under
arrest, and we were all under arrest. The
headquarters were demoralized and aban-
doned, and we could not answer any messages. The men went back to work, and the
ranks were broken up by the federal courts of
the United States.

The officials of the American Railway
Union realized that lawlessness would
destroy their cause, and for this reason
exerted every effort to keep the strike
free of such acts. In spite of all they
could do, violence occurred; but most of
it, as previous treatment has made abun-
dantly clear, was the work of lawless
elements over which the union could
exercise no control. The strikers were
nevertheless credited by an enraged press
and an inflamed public with full responsibility for all the mischief done — a
situation which made it easy for the government to employ boldly and without
restraint a weapon which otherwise

would have been used with greater
caution. The injunction was so sweeping
and all inclusive that the union leaders
could not move without running afoul of
it. The purpose of the writ was designed
not so much to protect property as to
crush the strike.

It is doubtful that labor realized the
full import of the injunction when first
issued, although Eugene Debs did consult some of the best constitutional
lawyers in Chicago. They told him to
proceed just as he had been doing, com-
mitting no violence and doing everything
in his power to restrain men from lawlessness. This Debs did, but he soon
discovered that the courts placed a construction upon the writ which left him
no freedom of action. That he did not
perceive the true character of the injunction when it was first served is evident by
the following observation which he made
on July 4:

I cannot see the necessity for serving an
injunction on me commanding me not to do
that which the statutes of the state also require me not to do. It is an assumption that
I am ignorant of the law. I again say that I
have done absolutely nothing prohibited by
the law. I shall not do so, nor will I coun-
tenance others doing so.

In seeking evidence that the injunction
had been violated, Milchrist urged the
general managers to report the names of
any who encouraged employees to strike
or who in any way sought to discourage
workers from performing their duty.
Significantly enough, the role played by
Thomas Milchrist in shaping the judicial
strategy was much less important than
that of Edwin Walker, in whose judgment the attorney-general seemed to re-
pose the most implicit confidence. As
special district attorney, Walker was pre-

pared to serve as liaison agent between the government and the railroads; and not only did he confer with railroad lawyers and executives whenever it suited his purpose, but he attended meetings of the General Managers' Association. In serving two masters he experienced little difficulty, since both sought the same broad objectives in the struggle.

From almost the very outset Walker favored both equity and criminal procedure against the strikers. Milchrist at first opposed the latter course because, as he claimed, it would be extremely difficult to obtain evidence for convictions; but, in the opinion of Walker, the mere calling of a grand jury and the securing of indictments would have a "greater restraining effect upon Debs and his followers than proceeding by injunction." On July 3 Edwin Walker outlined his plan of action to the attorney-general. Equity proceedings would have to await the gathering of further evidence; but, as was confidently expected, sufficient proof of contempt would be assembled within a few days, and then Debs and his associates would be sent to jail. It was further indicated that in one week a grand jury would be summoned to indict the strike leaders for conspiracy. Walker was careful, however, to emphasize the dangers of precipitate action but explained that, since he had a thorough understanding with Judge Grosscup, everything would proceed as rapidly and effectively as circumstances warranted. To Richard Olney this strategy seemed agreeable, although he was becoming impatient for action, and in reply he instructed the special assistant district attorney not to lose any time in calling a special session of the grand jury.

On July 6 Walker informed the attorney-general that sufficient evidence had now been gathered for presentation to the grand jury which was scheduled to meet on July 10. He expressed the belief that the bail would be so large in the aggregate that Debs and his associates would have to go to jail and remain there until their cases were called up for trial. Walker explained:

We shall be able to show that this conspiracy has extended over the entire northwest, as well as the Pacific coast, and also east through Michigan, Indiana and Ohio, and I firmly believe that the result of these trials and the punishment of the leaders will be so serious that a general strike upon any railroad will not again occur for a series of years.

The general managers seemed to think that the arrest of Eugene Debs was being needlessly delayed. This feeling Edwin Walker did not share, because of the belief that it would be inexpedient to arrest Debs before he was indicted and that contempt proceedings should await action by the grand jury. He felt that hasty action would prove dangerous and might influence the Knights of Labor to call a general strike. However logical may have been his position, the attorneys for the General Managers' Association assumed a very critical attitude in the matter. They believed that the sooner Debs was behind bars, the quicker the strike would collapse. On July 9 the president of the Chicago, Milwaukee, and St. Paul Railroad revealed the nature of these criticisms to Walker, who seemed to take them quite seriously. He decided to confer immediately with some of these lawyers, including the chairman of the legal committee of the General Managers' Association, and agreed to advise Milchrist to order the arrest of Debs if these attorneys should recommend such a course. What transpired at this conference is not known, but on the following day the grand jury assembled and took the action which Richard Olney and the general managers so fervently desired.

When Milchrist and Walker met the special grand jury on July 10, they asked for indictments against Eugene Debs and his co-officials on the grounds of conspiracy. Composed of out-of-town residents, the jury proved extremely amenable. In his instructions to this group Judge Grosscup smoothed the way for prompt action by leaving virtually no course open but the one demanded by the government. He pointed out that an agreement on the part of two or more individuals to stop trains unlawfully would have the effect of halting mail trains and interstate commerce, and this should be proof of the existence of a conspiracy. The railroads, he explained, have a right to the service of each employee until he lawfully decides to quit and that concerted action to induce men to strike "under any effective penalty or threat . . . . to the injury of the mail service or the prompt transportation of interstate commerce" might be classified as conspiracy.

With such advice the grand jury retired to hear evidence, which consisted principally of telegrams dispatched from the headquarters of the American Railway Union. The only witness was Edward M. Mulford, manager of the Western Union office in Chicago, who was subpoenaed to produce copies of these messages. At first he refused to make them available, on the grounds that, being "privileged communications," they should remain in the custody of his company. When Grosscup, however, threatened him with a jail sentence, he decided to yield to the will of the court.

Only the telegrams that seemed most incriminating were submitted to the jury. None advocated violence while some ad-

vised against it, but there were many which counseled the railroad workers to support the boycott. In view of what Judge Grosscup had said, such urgings were construed as evidence of conspiracy, and without delay the grand jury voted true bills for the four highest officials of the American Railway Union: President Eugene Debs, Vice-President George W. Howard, Secretary Sylvester Keliher, and Lewis W. Rogers, editor of the *Railway Times*. The jury was in session not more than two hours when this action was taken, and ten minutes later bench warrants were issued. With a speed that must have gladdened the hearts of Walker and Olney, the accused were quickly apprehended and brought into court. After a few hours of detention, they were released on bail, the bonds required for each being ten thousand dollars.

While Debs and his associates were in the custody of the court, the union headquarters were raided by a squad of deputy marshals and deputy post-office inspectors. Every room was completely ransacked; and all books, papers, records, and correspondence, including the unopened personal mail of Eugene Debs, were seized and transferred to the office of the United States district attorney. Although conducted according to instructions from Thomas Milchrist, the raid was in complete violation of the subpoena issued for the occasion – a court order which merely required that the private secretary of Debs and certain other persons appear before the grand jury with the books and papers of the union. There was no authority to make any arrests or seizures. Realizing the illegality of the action, Judge Grosscup quickly repudiated it and ordered all private papers returned. . . .

The attorney-general viewed this raid

as embarrassing to the government. On July 11 he bluntly reminded Walker that the seizure of Debs's papers was unlawful and that they should be returned and the affair publicly disavowed. Olney was careful to explain that, in enforcing the law, the government could not itself afford to be lawless by violating personal rights. . . .

Convinced that the strike leaders feared the grand jury more than the presence of troops, the prosecution made the greatest possible use of this jury. Numerous arrests were made during the rioting in Chicago, and those who could not furnish bail were committed to jail. The grand jury indicted many of these and in all named sixty-nine persons in the omnibus indictments for conspiracy. Seven indictments were voted against Debs, Howard, and Rogers, but only three each against the full board of directors. So enthusiastic was the jury in probing the situation that Milchrist and Walker experienced some difficulty in confining the jury's work strictly to offenses against the transportation of mail and commerce. On July 19 the jury completed its investigation and was discharged.

Elsewhere throughout the United States grand juries were summoned and numerous indictments for conspiracy drawn up, some of which were directed against large groups of strikers. . . . Among the hundreds arrested for contempt, only a very small proportion was actually found guilty. Erroneous arrests were to be expected in a struggle characterized by such tenseness; but it may be assumed that the general policy of making arrests represented a part of the strategy of the Department of Justice to undermine the morale of labor. According to the vice-president of the American Railway Union, the practice of the government in this respect was most objectionable.

Men have been arrested in Chicago because they refused to turn switches when told to; they were arrested when they refused to get on an engine and fire an engine; one man was arrested for going up and looking at a policeman's star; in Albuquerque, New Mexico, they arrested a man and he was sentenced to fifteen days in jail for contempt of court because he refused to get on an engine and fire it when told; the fact that he did not get on the engine was considered contempt of court.

Before the special grand jury in Chicago had completed its work, contempt proceedings were commenced. On July 17 two informations were filed in the federal district court against Debs, Howard, Keliher, and Rogers: one by George R. Peck in behalf of the receivers of the Santa Fe Road, and the other by Milchrist and Walker in behalf of the United States government. The defendants were charged with contempt and their immediate arrest demanded. The prosecution declared that the injunction of Judges Grosscup and Woods had been wilfully and deliberately violated by Debs and his co-officials, not once, but on numerous occasions. It was alleged that in open disregard of the writ, the defendants by telegram had continued to urge railroad employees on various lines to quit work. Hundreds of such messages were dispatched and many employees were induced to strike, often in a body, thus causing serious interference to the movement of interstate commerce. The government further charged that the strikers seized railroad property, fostered violence, and by physical force obstructed mail and interstate trains. Workers who refused to join the strike were intimidated. By this and other means the union was charged with seeking to establish unlawfully a boycott of Pullman sleepers. The prosecution contended that the directors of the American Railway Union possessed full authority to call the workers out on a strike and by the exercise of this power had flagrantly violated the injunction.

In seeking to prove contempt the government submitted some telegrams to the court. When only a few had been read, the judge announced that sufficient evidence had been presented to indicate a deliberate violation of the injunction. The attorney for the American Railway Union, S. S. Gregory, vainly protested that the information failed to charge the defendants with personal participation in any violence and that the case as presented did not warrant jurisdiction by a court of equity. The government, he announced, was really using its power and authority to vindicate the property rights of the railroads. The judge, however, could see no need for further discussion at this time and ordered the arrest of the defendants but suspended service of the writs when assured that the accused would voluntarily surrender themselves. This Debs and his three associates did at the afternoon session of the court. Again Gregory endeavored to save his clients by declaring that if time permitted he could prove that the information failed to show any violation of the injunction and that until contempt had been proved there could be no punishment. He explained it was no offense for workers to quit work peacefully; and as for the allegation that threats and intimidation had been used by the accused — there was nothing in the information to bear this out.

Although unimpressed by these arguments, the court was willing to grant the defense sufficient time to answer the

informations and accordingly deferred the hearing until July 23. This was done over the strenuous objections of Edwin Walker, who, being anxious to get away for his summer vacation, demanded an immediate hearing. . . .

As scheduled, the hearing for contempt began on July 23, with Judges Grosscup and Woods presiding. The four defendants, each wearing a new white ribbon, appeared without showing any trace of their imprisonment. Gregory, who was now assisted by another attorney, W. W. Erwin, filed a joint answer to the contempt charges. All the allegations set forth by Milchrist and Walker were categorically denied. The defendants disclaimed any intention of violating the restraining order and emphatically declared that they had not done so. It was pointed out that the workers on each railroad, by a majority vote, alone possessed the power to call a strike and that the high officials of the union might advise but could exercise no authority in the matter. . . . The court sustained the prosecution by refusing to dismiss contempt proceedings or to permit a jury to hear the case. Before the hearing could progress further, however, Edwin Walker became ill, and the court decided on July 25 to postpone the case until September 5. . . .

Walker felt certain that labor considered the contempt proceedings as a test case involving the effectiveness of equity in controlling unions. In view of this he believed that the defendants would contest the case, if possible, even more strenuously than the indictments for conspiracy. The need for a government victory in the matter seemed imperative to him; and to Olney he explained: "If the courts sustain the position of the government, that equity has jurisdiction to restrain such confederations, and enforce the rule of non-interference with the transportation of the mails and interstate commerce, there would be no more boycotting, and no further violence, in aid of strikes. . . .

Clarence Darrow was invited to join in the defense of the accused and after some hesitation accepted, although aware that it would take a tremendous amount of time with little compensation. He did so out of sympathy for labor and because of the belief that the leaders of the American Railway Union were being unjustly prosecuted. When the strike broke out, he was counsel for the Chicago and Northwestern Railroad and was assigned to the legal committee of the General Managers' Association. Having no desire to be a party in the campaign to crush the strikers, he asked to be relieved of this responsibility. The president of the railroad, to whom Darrow explained his position so candidly, very generously permitted the lawyer to remain in the service of the road without having to use his talents against labor. Later, when Darrow decided to defend the officials of the American Railway Union, he was granted leave from his duties on this road. . . .

In the federal court at Chicago on September 5 William A. Woods, as presiding judge, began the hearing on contempt. The defense was represented by Erwin, Darrow, and Gregory, and the government by Walker and Milchrist. . . .

As the hearing progressed, it became apparent that the defense was pursuing a course at variance with what the government expected. Not only did the defendants avail themselves of the privilege not to testify, but they called no witnesses and offered no evidence in their behalf except parts of certain documents which were offered in connection with other parts presented by the prosecution. Such

a policy was doubtless dictated by the belief that it would be better strategy to save their witnesses and most of their evidence for the conspiracy trial, considered much more crucial. The counsel for the defense also may have questioned the wisdom of revealing their full case in a court where there was no jury and before a judge whose lack of sympathy for labor was mirrored in the injunction which he had helped to issue.

The defense was, nevertheless, emphatic in denying that there had been any violation of the injunction. It was contended that the defendants did not favor interference with the movement of mail or interstate commerce, nor did they at any time urge the strikers to engage in lawlessness. The right of the court to issue the writ and to hear and determine the contempt case was seriously questioned. The court, it was held, had no authority under the Sherman Anti-trust Act to issue the injunction. The denial of trial by jury and the punishment of the accused for conspiracy and contempt — thus twice for the same offense — were declared to be unconstitutional.

In seeking to prove guilt the prosecution called numerous witnesses, most of whom were furnished by the railroads; and in addition submitted much documentary material, principally telegrams. As the hearing proceeded, Walker kept Olney well informed of developments and was in turn advised by the attorney-general. Walker acknowledged to Olney on the fourteenth of September that the defendants "did not personally or physically interfere with the movement of trains" and that they did "expressly warn all persons against violence and interference with the transportation of the mails." In the opinion of Walker, however, this fact did not lessen their guilt. As the railroads were being paralyzed and as disorders were spreading, he explained, the accused continued to dispatch orders "calling the men out and urging those who were not members of the union to join the strike." Walker confided to Olney the belief that, if the court should deny the legality of the injunction under the Sherman Anti-trust Act, the government could still invoke the writ to prevent unlawful interference with the transportation of the mail.

In the judgment of Richard Olney, the Sherman Anti-trust Law furnished the necessary authority for the writ; but, even without resort to this measure, the government was still able to protect the mail by equity proceedings. He believed, however, that the injunction could be sustained on broader grounds – the right of a court of equity to render protection against a public nuisance. In clarifying this point Olney explained to Walker that a railroad was nothing but "a peculiar species of a public highway" and that, if the courts could enjoin any obstruction or obstacle on a public highway, they could do the same for any railroad. By virtue of the Interstate Commerce Act, declared the attorney-general, all interstate railroads were subject to the jurisdiction of the United States, and any obstruction thereon could be enjoined by the federal government as a public nuisance. Nor did the obstruction necessarily have to be some physical obstacle; it could be a strike. By uniting the workers and simultaneously withdrawing them from an interstate railroad, the defendants obstructed the operation of the road and were guilty of creating a public nuisance. Such an action, averred Olney, was illegal and could be restrained by a court of equity. Realizing the effectiveness of this connection, Walker gave it considerable emphasis in his closing arguments, without, however, overlook-

ing the Sherman Anti-trust Act as a source of authority for the writ.

Since Judge Woods viewed the Debs contempt case as a real opportunity, he was in no hurry to hand down the decision, which he desired to be an extremely able piece of work. Although the final arguments were heard during the latter part of September, it was not until December 14 that the decision was rendered. In all respects it was a sweeping victory for the government. Every contention of the prosecution was sustained; and by numerous legal citations Woods endeavored to buttress his conclusions.

Concerning the applicability of the Sherman Anti-trust Act to this case, the judge entertained not the slightest doubt. . . . The right to punish for contempt was held not to be an abridgment of the right of trial by jury. . . . Did the defendants violate the injunction? In the opinion of the court they did. . . . As for the admonitions against violence – these the judge was disposed to discount, expressing the belief that they were primarily designed to win public support for labor. . . .

Eugene Debs was sentenced by Judge Woods to six months' confinement, while the other defendants were given only three. Because of crowded conditions at the Cook County jail it was decided to commit the prisoners to the McHenry County jail at Woodstock, Illinois, where on January 8, 1895, they began serving their sentences for contempt. Shortly thereafter the counsel for the defense applied to the United States Supreme Court for a writ of error and a writ of habeas corpus. While denying the former, the court consented to grant a hearing on the latter, which, however, was not held until March 26.

In pleading their case before this

high tribunal, the defense counsel was strengthened by the addition of a distinguished statesman and lawyer, Lyman Trumbull, whose services were offered without compensation, although he did accept traveling expenses. . . .

In addition to Trumbull, the petitioners were represented by Darrow and Gregory. The latter, in his arguments, explained that the Sherman Anti-trust Act was not applicable, but that, if it were, then Section 4, which authorizes such proceedings, was unconstitutional. Why? Because it committed to a court of equity the enforcement of a penal statute and denied to the accused trial by jury contrary to the Sixth Amendment. Gregory contended that

no more tyrannous and arbitrary government can be devised than the administration of criminal law by a single judge by means of injunction and proceedings in contempt. To extend this power generally to criminal cases would be absolutely destructive to liberty and intolerable to a free people. It would be worse than *ex post facto* legislation. No man could be safe; no limits could be prescribed to the acts which might be forbidden nor the punishment to be inflicted.

In denying that the prisoners had engaged in any conspiracy, Lyman Trumbull argued that what they did was done to compel the Pullman Company to adopt a conciliatory policy toward its employees. It was for this purpose only that the American Railway Union launched the boycott and then urged its members to quit work on the railroads which persisted in operating Pullman cars. In pursuit of this lawful purpose, declared Trumbull, Eugene Debs and his associates are charged with obstructing commerce, but "refusing to work for a railroad is no crime, and, though such action may incidentally delay the mails or interfere with interstate commerce, it being a lawful act, and not done for the purpose, it is no offense." Relative to the injunction, the attorney flatly charged that it pertained to matters over which a court of equity has no jurisdiction. In clarifying this point, he explained that a restraining order could be used by a property-owner to protect himself against an "irreparable injury" but that it was contrary to time-honored practice for the government to invoke the writ to prevent interference with private property, even though it were done to safeguard interstate commerce. If the prisoners are guilty of interfering with the transportation of the mails, asserted Trumbull, they should be punished under the criminal statutes, but under no circumstances does an equity court have jurisdiction.

Clarence Darrow contended that the prisoners were entitled to freedom because the court lacked authority to issue the injunction and because the acts complained of in the information were not illegal. Concerning the first point, Darrow probed very carefully the history of the Sherman Anti-trust Act. By analyzing the disposition of Congress at the time the bill was passed, he tried to prove that the law was intended to apply only to "combinations in the shape of trusts and pools." He revealed that at no place in the measure was "there any mention of any labor organization or strike or boycott or the slightest reference that would be construed by men of ordinary intelligence as an intention to apply this law to the combinations of laboring men, or strikes or boycotts." And yet, protested Darrow, the circuit court dared to use such a law as authority for the injunction.

Relative to his second major contention, he sought to show that the defendants did not violate the injunction, nor did they do anything which the courts had the right to enjoin. It was pointed out that the telegrams dispatched by Debs and his co-officials furnished virtually the only allegation in the information pertinent to the violation of the injunction. Some of these dispatches urged the members of the American Railway Union to quit work and to induce others to do so. In prevailing upon the workers to follow such a course, Debs was merely exercising a right which the courts had recognized as belonging to labor. "The whole information," emphasized Darrow, "plainly shows that since the granting of the injunction not one act was committed by these defendants, or any of them, that was in any way unlawful, or that could be forbidden by the court if workingmen are to have the right to organize and the right to strike."

It was denied that the disorders which occurred during the strike were even remotely perpetrated by the American Railway Union. No evidence was presented, not one single fact, proclaimed Darrow, to show that the union or any of its officials were connected with any unlawful acts. Just because disorders occurred during the strike, he exclaimed, is no reason why the defendants should be held responsible. He further said:

If men could not do lawful acts because violence might possibly or reasonably result, then the most innocent deeds might be crimes. To make men responsible for the remote consequences of their acts would be to destroy individual liberty and make men slaves. . . . If it is lawful for men to organize and in accordance with the organization to cease labor, they cannot be regarded as criminals because violence, bloodshed or crime follows such a strike. . . . Strikes are deplorable, and so are their causes. All men who engage in them hope for a time when better social relations will make them as

unnecessary as any other form of warfare will some day be. But under the present conditions of industrial life, with the present conflicting interests of capital and labor, each perhaps blindly seeking for more perfect social adjustments, strikes and lockouts are incidents of industrial life. They are not justified because men love social strife and industrial war, but because in the present system of industrial evolution to deprive workingmen of this power would be to strip and bind them and leave them helpless as the prey of the great and strong.

The government was represented by Attorney-General Olney, Assistant Attorney-General Whitney, and Edwin Walker. So important did Richard Olney consider the case that, contrary to his policy, he appeared before the tribunal. The only other time he did this, while serving as attorney-general, was in arguing the income tax case. He was determined that the contempt decision should be sustained. His feeling for Debs was one of unmitigated hatred. Olney was extremely anxious that this labor leader be severely punished; but in a communication to Walker on January 7, 1895, he expressed the fear that "no punishment he is likely to get, if he is convicted and sentenced on all the pending indictments, will be commensurate with his offense."

Reserving for himself a major role in the hearing, Olney argued eloquently that the injunction should rest upon broader grounds than were set forth in the circuit court decision. While convinced that complete authority for the writ was furnished by the Sherman Antitrust Act and by the government's property interest in the mail bags, he nevertheless believed a much better basis for the injunction existed, and to this proposition devoted the greater part of his plea. The federal government, he announced, had complete jurisdiction over the railroads by virtue of the interstate commerce law and other acts relating to post roads and the shipment of livestock. This legislation was construed by Olney to constitute an express prohibition against interference with interstate rail transportation. Notwithstanding, many railroads were paralyzed, and much property was destroyed in July, 1894, the responsibility for which, in his judgment, belonged to the defendants, unless "it be true that man can wantonly touch the match to powder and yet be blameless because not rightly realizing the ensuing devastation." In meeting the situation, explained the attorney-general, the state authorities acted slowly and ineffectively, thus aggravating the situation. But, even if Illinois had done otherwise, he averred, there was need for intervention by the United States government, since interstate commerce — a federal matter — was being assaulted.

What remedies did the government have? Irrespective of the Sherman Antitrust Act, the United States could prosecute for conspiracy to obstruct the mails; but this method, he revealed, would not be very effective against large mobs, since the object was not so much to punish interference as to prevent it. The government could apply to the courts of equity for a restraining order against unlawful interruption of interstate rail transportation, and in doing so, insisted Olney, the government had no alternative because criminal prosecution was wholly inadequate in meeting the emergency. Just as a trustee has the right to protect the property intrusted to his care by resort to a court of equity, even though he has no private interest in the matter, so the United States — a trustee for all interests and parties concerned — was held to possess the power to render protection by all the means at its disposal,

including equity proceedings. It was denied that the government needed expressed authorization from Congress to avail itself of this weapon. The executive branch of the government had received statutory power to protect interstate commerce and was under obligation "to carry the legislation into effect by all appropriate means at its command." Since the injunction was the most effective instrumentality in this case, Olney held that it was precisely the one which the government, as the guardian of public interests and rights, should employ. Contempt proceedings, he pointed out, were essentially of a summary character requiring no indictment by grand jury or trial by petit jury. As to the charge that the defendants had been deprived of their constitutional rights, he pointed out that the same act may be a crime and yet involve contempt.

. . . The hearing required only two days, but not until May 27 did Justice Brewer deliver the unanimous opinion of the Supreme Court. . . .

The court denied that the right of employees to quit work had been challenged. The purpose of the writ was rather "to restrain forcible obstructions of the highway along which interstate commerce travels and the mails are carried." Convinced that there was such an obstruction, the Supreme Court held that the circuit court possessed the authority to issue the injunction and to punish by fine or imprisonment all who were guilty of disobeying the order. The writ of habeas corpus was thus denied and the decision of Judge Woods affirmed, but on broader grounds than had been advanced by the lower court.

In the judgment of Richard Olney, the decision left nothing to be desired; and by the business interests throughout the nation it was received with unconcealed enthusiasm. . . . None seemed more jubilant than George R. Peck, chairman of the legal committee of the General Managers' Association, who wired the attorney-general: "I congratulate you with all my heart on the Debs Decision. The Supreme Court seems to agree with you that 'the soil of Illinois is the soil of the United States.'"

The decision proved offensive to workers everywhere. Its implications were all too clear, particularly as to the extraordinary power now recognized as available to the government in resisting the efforts of organized labor. The injunction had received from the Supreme Court a legal sanctity such as it had never had before. It is little wonder that this decision, coming as it did close upon the heels of the income tax ruling, caused many people to view that high tribunal as an exalted servant of the vested interests. . . .

. . . Four months earlier, or sixteen days after the defendants started serving their sentence for contempt, the trial for conspiracy began in the federal court of Judge Grosscup. From the Woodstock jail, some fifty miles northwest of Chicago, Debs and his fellow-prisoners were taken daily to that city for the trial which opened on January 24. The directors of the American Railway Union were not the only ones accused of conspiracy to obstruct and retard the mails. Originally sixty-nine had been indicted for this offense by the federal grand jury in Chicago, but the government decided, prior to the commencement of the trial, to proceed against only forty-five — a number which was shortly reduced to twenty.

The attorneys for the defense consisted of Clarence Darrow and S. S. Gregory, while the prosecution comprised Edwin Walker, Thomas Milchrist, and the new federal district attorney, John C. Black.

As the trial got under way, it became apparent to all that this was no ordinary case but one having far-reaching significance to labor. In the opinion of Darrow, it was a historical case — one which would count much for liberty or against liberty. The punishment for conspiracy carried a maximum penalty of two years' imprisonment or a fine of ten thousand dollars or both; but to Darrow it was not just a question of securing an acquittal for the defendants but of safeguarding the rights of labor. . . .

Farmers predominated in the jury, which was selected with a minimum of delay. The government was careful to see that all workingmen were excluded but the jury as constituted did not appear prejudiced against labor. Having disposed of the preliminaries, the court was now prepared for a statement from the prosecution and the defense.

Speaking in behalf of the former, Milchrist charged that the violence during the strike was the result of the conspiracy entered into by the defendants. In proving conspiracy, he denied that it was necessary to show that any of the accused had committed an overt act or that they had met together or formally organized for the purpose of carrying out the conspiracy. He declared that, since those who engage in conspiracy do so in secret, it would be impossible to prove it by direct evidence and that the "results of their acts must be taken as evidence of their intentions." The defendants, he charged, were guilty of conspiracy when they cut off Pullman cars which comprised a regular part of the trains carrying mail. Milchrist conceded that it was lawful for Debs to call out members of the American Railway Union but that in ordering others out he was guilty of conspiracy.

Clarence Darrow in opening the case

for the defense charged that Milchrist was a "puppet in the hands of the great railroad corporations in this persecution, not prosecution." In the three thousand dollars' worth of telegrams sent by the defendants, not one, it was affirmed, contained a word urging violence, although many exhorted the strikers to avoid lawlessness. No person, averred Darrow, can be convicted of conspiracy unless it is proved that he conspired to do the acts complained of; but Milchrist, refusing to recognize this, has contended that the accused conducted a strike during which lawlessness occurred, and that they are therefore responsible for it. It was explained that there were "two requisites to crime, intent and act" and that, in so far as the mail was concerned, there was not the slightest desire on the part of the defendants to interfere; indeed, they were anxious to haul the mails but would not allow the operation of Pullman cars. The general managers, on the contrary, refused to permit the mail to move without these cars, preferring, as Darrow revealed, "to use the inconvenience of the public and the feeling of sanctity for the mails as a club to defeat the effort that was being made to better the condition of workingmen and women."

Darrow reminded the court that the right to strike has been acknowledged by the prosecution. The railroad workers, availing themselves of this right, quit work and very soon became engaged in a struggle of gigantic proportions. "Yet great as was the excitement stirred up by the fevered accounts of a fevered time," said Darrow, "scarcely any foolish words and not a single unlawful one can be charged to these men." He further declared: "The evidence will show that all the defendants did was in behalf of the employees of that man whose name is odious wherever men have a drop of blood, Mr. Pullman. No man or newspaper undertook to defend Mr. Pullman except the General Managers' Association, and their defense gives added proof of his infamy."

In his interpretation of what comprised conspiracy, Judge Grosscup gave considerable comfort to the prosecution. In proving conspiracy it was necessary, he ruled, to "show an agreement of obstruction which is to retard the United States mails." In elucidating this, he expressed the belief that the government did not have to show that the agreement in so many words provided for interference with the mails. If the agreement did not infer obstruction but had the logical effect of causing interference with the mail — this would be an agreement of conspiracy. If the government, declared the judge, could prove that the defendants "had entered into an agreement unlawfully to stop all trains, and the natural and the logical and almost inevitable effect was the stoppage of the mail trains, such an agreement . . . might be sufficient proof of the existence of the conspiracy."

As the trial progressed, numerous witnesses were summoned to testify. Edward M. Mulford, manager of Western Union in Chicago, revealed that nine thousand telegrams with Debs's signature were dispatched during the strike. The most outstanding witness was Eugene Debs, who traced the part which the American Railway Union played in the strike. The origin, character, and aims of the union were set forth, as he endeavored to prove that it was scrupulously committed to a strict obedience of the law. There was nothing spectacular or sensational in his remarks, only a calm and dispassionate recital of the facts.

George Pullman might have proved an interesting witness, had he been willing to testify. On February 6 the court issued a subpoena for him, but the deputy marshal, in calling at the Pullman Building to serve the writ, was informed, after some delay, that George Pullman was out. Thirty minutes previously, as the usher in the reception room later testified on the witness stand, George Pullman entered his office. When informed of the deputy's mission, however, Pullman quickly gave instructions that he was not in and by another exit hastily left the office and soon afterward the city. It was not until after the jury had been dismissed that he returned to Chicago and, accompanied by his attorney, Robert Todd Lincoln, called upon Judge Grosscup. Presumably the entire matter was quietly and amicably adjusted.

Among the witnesses were several railroad executives, but their testimony was not nearly so sensational as the minutes of the General Managers' Association, a copy of which Darrow managed to obtain. Using the document as evidence, he tried to show that the railroads had united in a powerful confederation for the purpose of uniformly reducing wages and otherwise pursuing a common policy toward labor.

The progress of the trial was suddenly halted on February 8 by the illness of one of the jury. Being satisfied with developments, the defense was eager that some arrangement be made to resume the trial. It was proposed that a new jury be immediately impaneled, consisting of the eleven old jurors and one other, and that the evidence already taken be read to them. The judge, however, was inclined to question the legality of such procedure, and accordingly dismissed the jury on February 12. This was done over the strenuous objections of the defense, which was convinced that the jury was growing more and more sympathetic to their side. According to Darrow, the jury, when discharged, stood eleven to one for acquittal. Convinced of the futility of prosecuting the accused, the district attorney continued the case for a year and then quietly entered nolle prosequi on the records, thus indicating that no further action would be taken.

After the abrupt ending of the conspiracy case, Eugene Debs still had the greater part of his contempt sentence to serve. . . . The months of imprisonment gave him the opportunity to read widely and to meditate deeply on the injustices and contradictions of the economic system. Slowly a transformation occurred in his mental processes; and, when he emerged from prison, he was unalterably committed to socialism as the only hope of mankind. To that cause he was thenceforth destined to devote the best years of his life.

The imprisonment of Debs had the further effect of making him a national character and in labor and liberal circles somewhat of a martyr. His mail at Woodstock was exceptionally heavy and when freed he was in demand almost everywhere as a public speaker. His release was the occasion for a mammoth celebration in Chicago by organized labor. Representatives of more than fifty unions journeyed in a special train to Woodstock in order to greet their hero and accompany him to Chicago. Upon their return, Debs was welcomed at the station by one hundred thousand people. Declining to ride in a carriage drawn by six white horses, he expressed a preference to walk in the parade held in his honor. That night he received a tremendous ovation in the great convention hall at Battery D, which overflowed with admirers and supporters. Among the speakers was Henry D. Lloyd, who hailed Debs as the "most popular man among the real people today . . . the

victim of judicial lynch law, the repudi-
ator of contempt of court as a substitute
for the constitution of the United States,
and of Gatling guns as harmonizer of
labour and capital; the first rebel against
government by injunction.". . .

. . . As the years slipped by and the
memories of the Pullman Strike grew
dimmer and dimmer, it became abun-
dantly clear that labor had not suffered
irreparably in that struggle. Fourteen
years had elapsed when there appeared
in the *Journal of the Switchmen's Union*
an article in retrospect. . . .

There have been many changes since that
great struggle against slavery, degradation
and privation. . . . Labor unions have again
become . . . stronger than ever. Many an
honest workingman and woman went hungry
in 1894 for daring to rebel against the hu-
miliating conditions that existed at Pullman.
Many a union man went to jail for disobeying
the injunction of Judges Grosscup, Woods
and Taft, but today we find Pullman has
passed to the Great Beyond, where all are
supposed to be equal; Woods is dead; Cleveland is dead; Egan has disappeared to God
knows where; Grosscup has been under
indictment; St. John has passed into the
shadowy valley, but Eugene Debs still lives,
loved by his fellowmen because of his honesty, for his many sacrifices to the cause of
humanity. The cause of the working class is
still here and here to stay and will be crowned
gloriously triumphant long after the oppressors and tyrants and all their fawning retain-
ers have gone the way of flesh and passed
from memory.

From 1894 on, labor strove diligently
to circumscribe the use of the injunction
and otherwise to secure from legislative
bodies a fair measure of protection
against judicial and corporate tyranny.
The odds were great, but the forces of
labor persisted. In 1896 the Democratic
party protested against the arbitrary interference by federal authorities in local
affairs and denounced "government by
injunction as a new and highly dangerous
form of oppression by which Federal
Judges in contempt of the laws of the
states and the rights of citizens, become
at once legislators, judges and executioners." It was not, however, until the
adoption of the Clayton Anti-trust Act
in 1914 that labor unions received some
measure of protection from the injunction and were expressly exempted from
the operation of the Sherman Anti-trust
Act. The right to strike, picket, and boycott was held not to violate any federal
law. Although these gains were gratifying, they were subsequently reduced in
value by judicial interpretation. Un-
daunted, labor fought on and in time
was able to implement this law and
obtain other vital pro-labor enactments
— until at length the workers had gained
far more legislative protection and assistance than the strike-weary men of 1894
could have dreamed was possible. In the
matter of settling railroad disputes, extraordinary progress was likewise made,
although the compulsory plan of arbitration, which the Strike Commission
advocated, was never destined to gain
acceptance.

In scrutinizing the tremendous gains
achieved by labor since that strife-ridden
year of 1894, it is not possible to say with
finality that any part of them had its
origin in the Pullman Strike. But certainly from that struggle impulses were
set in motion which affected the whole
course of labor history. The Pullman
Strike was more than just an industrial
clash; it was an upheaval which shook
the nation to its very depths and led to
extraordinary applications of old laws
and the creation of highly effective anti-
labor weapons. In the heat of the
struggle precedents were established that

required long years to nullify. From that crisis labor gained rich experience and learned valuable lessons. In seeking the more abundant life, the workers were becoming more and more determined to secure for themselves a fairer share from the fruits of their toil.

In the face of overwhelming defeat the American Railway Union expressed no murmur of despair and no regret for its part in the drama. The cause, for which so much had been given and from which so little had been asked, was now finished. The men had fought well and suffered much. Were their sacrifices in vain and the struggle a catastrophic loss to labor? The American Railway Union did not choose to think so. With perhaps a greater measure of truth than was then realized, this union bravely proclaimed: "No, it was not a defeat — this ending of the most momentous strike of modern times. It could not be, when we are so near a century that is to surely see the rights of the masses take that place in the policies of nations which is now basely devoted to the privileges of classes."

Suggestions for Additional Reading

Those who desire a more complete analysis of the Pullman strike and boycott, and of the attitudes of its participants, may wish to consult the United States Strike Commission: *Report on the Chicago Strike, June–July, 1894* (Washington, 1895). The Strike Commission, appointed by President Cleveland, held hearings in Chicago immediately at the close of the dispute. Testimony was received from the major participants and from the principal law-enforcement agents. After a thorough and well-conducted investigation, a comprehensive report was prepared by the Commission. A carefully documented account of the many facets of this dispute, which is sympathetic to labor, has been written by Almont Lindsey, *The Pullman Strike* (Chicago, 1942). It includes an excellent bibliography. Especially valuable chapters are those on the role of public opinion in the strike and on its political repercussions. Mention should also be made of a valuable contemporary account of the events at Pullman by the pastor of the First M. E. Church of Pullman, William H. Carwardine (*The Pullman Strike*, Chicago, 1894). Donald L. McMurry has written an important discussion of *Labor Policies of the General Managers' Association of Chicago, 1886–1894* in the Journal of Economic History, Vol. XIII, No. 2, 1953.

Among the biographies of the principal contestants are Allan Nevins' *Grover Cleveland: A Study in Courage* (New York, 1934), *Richard Olney and His Public Service* by Henry James (Boston, 1923), *"Eagle Forgotten": The Life of John Peter Altgeld* by Harry Barnard (New York, 1938), and Ray Ginger's *The Bending Cross: A Biography of Eugene Victor Debs* (New Brunswick, N. J., 1949). McAlister Coleman's *Eugene V. Debs* (New York, 1930) and *Debs: His Life, Writings and Speeches* (Chicago, 1908) should also be noted. Clarence Darrow's account of his association with the Debs case provides some interesting sidelights (*The Story of My Life*, New York, 1932). It suffers, however, from some serious lapses in memory.

Varying interpretations of the Pullman strike as a chapter in American labor history are to be found in Norman J. Ware's *Labor in Modern Industrial Society* (Boston, 1935), Chapter XIII; Selig Perlman, *A History of Trade Unionism in the United States* (New York, 1922), chapters VI and VII; and Harry W. Laidler, *Boycotts and the Labor Struggle* (New York, 1913), pages 100–108. A brief, overdramatic account of the Pullman episode is given in Chapter XI of Louis Adamic's *Dynamite: The Story of Class Violence in America* (New York, rev. ed., 1935).

A history of the labor injunction is presented in Felix Frankfurter and Nathan Greene, *The Labor Injunction* (New York, 1930). Another excellent study of the injunction is to be found in Edward Berman, *Labor and the Sherman Act* (New York, 1930). Charles O. Gregory, *Labor and the Law* (New York, rev. ed., 1949) also gives a lively account of the legal history of unionism. Chapters IV and V are of particular value.